Turn Your Workplace Into a **WOWplace**®!

Turn Your Workplace Into a **WOWplace**®!

*5 Rules for Going From OW! To **WOW**!*

Sandy Geroux

WOWplace International, LLC/Orlando, FL

Sandy Geroux/**WOWplace** International, LLC
Orlando, FL
www.the**WOWplace**.com

For general information about our other products and services, please contact Sandy Geroux at (407) 856-1188 or sandy@the**WOWplace**.com.

Turn Your Workplace Into a **WOWplace**/Sandy Geroux -- 1st ed.
ISBN 978-0-9788269-9-4

Thank you, Mom & Dad, for teaching me the values to treat others with respect and compassion.

Thank you, Bruce, for sharing and supporting everything I have done for the last 31 years. I can't wait to share many more years with you.

Thank you, Mark Wahlton, for taking the book to a new level with your keen eye and fresh perspective as you edited my words and made them stronger.

Workplace or WOWplace

Workplace

a place where **EMPLOYEES**

HAVE to go because they make a **PAYCHECK**.

WOWplace

a place where **PEOPLE**

LOVE to go because they make a **DIFFERENCE**!

CONTENTS

Preface

There are places that make us feel great every time we visit or even just call them. Sometimes we know exactly what makes us feel that way; other times we may not be able to identify it, but something's definitely there. It's in the way the place looks and feels, the way everyone who works there treats us and, just as importantly, the way they treat each other. The place is clean and neat, associates know what they're doing and seem happy to do it, and there's an air of camaraderie and respect that just doesn't exist everywhere.

This doesn't mean everything is perfect. Just like the rest of us, they're still dealing with human beings and humans aren't perfect, so these places have their issues, too. But they work through their challenges quickly and respectfully to all parties. Leaders openly respect their workers, and workers respect their leaders because of it. These companies have created an atmosphere of trust and appreciation where associates want to create **WOW**s for each other and are rewarded for doing so. This atmosphere spills over into the customer environment, as associates are inspired to treat customers the same way.

It is when all of this comes together and adds up to a whole lot of **WOW** for associates and customers alike that we realize we've created a **WOWplace**.

WOWplaces don't just happen by accident. They are created out of careful and deliberate planning, training and execution with the ultimate goal of creating and sustaining a culture that is focused on and delivers what is most important to every human being: the desire to be valued, listened to and respected.

We have all seen companies that are great to work for; then a new person or two comes in and everything changes . . . for the worse. As a result, one by one, the caring and compassionate people begin to leave until no one is left except those who either tolerate the bad behavior of the new associates or become like them. We've also seen the reverse, where a company may not have the most competitive wages or benefits, but the people and the important work they are committed to doing make it all worthwhile . . . and they stay.

That is because making a place great is not about "flash" or power; it's not even about money. It's about the way we communicate and interact with each other and let others know they are valued, listened to and appreciated.

It's about VALUES.
It's about TRUST.
It's about RESPECT.
It's about COMMITMENT to an ideal.
In essence, it's about CARING.

It's about caring more about others than about yourself – not to your detriment, but certainly more with their benefit in mind than your own.

The Amazing Impact of Caring About Others

Have you seen the YouTube video about the Piano Stairs? At a subway station in Stockholm, Sweden, it was observed that the people climbing the stairs were far outnumbered by those making the easier but much less healthy choice of taking the escalator. The question was posed, *"Could people be encouraged to engage in healthier behavior by making it fun?"*

To put this question to the test, an initiative was commissioned by Volkswagen to install a set of "piano keys" on the stairs by attaching sensors to the stairs and covering them with white and black materials in a pattern that resembled the keys of a piano. When anyone stepped on a sensor, a sound was played that corresponded with the sound of the piano key being stepped on. Climbing the stairs played a musical scale.

This was so interesting to look at, and so much fun to try, that 66 percent more people began climbing the stairs versus taking the escalator! Video footage actually showed people engaging in their normal behavior pattern by heading for the escalator, and upon noticing the stairs, turning away from the escalator and climbing the stairs instead.

Lone walkers climbed the stairs; parents helped children climb the stairs; pet owners climbed the stairs with their pets. People climbed the stairs in pairs, "playing tunes" together as they went – some even jumped and danced together on the stairs to have more fun together! Everyone laughed, smiled and encouraged each other to engage in new and healthier behaviors because they were having so much fun doing it!

Volkswagen's objective in creating this initiative was to help people engage in activities that would improve their lives – in this case, get more exercise. Done solely for the purpose of helping others and creating fun, an added benefit for Volkswagen was that the brand was brought to mind in a fun and positive way due to their concern for the population at large. This cannot help but enhance their image, and could positively affect their sales and profits, as well.

This concept can be translated to the workplace. If people are having fun and enjoying their workplace, they are inspired to encourage others to have as much fun as *they* are having, even going so far as to help them do so. Conversely, if they hate their jobs, hate the people they work with and are generally miserable at work, they are "inspired" to help others be as miserable as they are – proving the old adage that *"misery loves company."*

As a society, we spend a lot of time and effort thinking and talking about the need to make things better. It is time for each of us to take personal responsibility to commit to doing something about it. It is time for us to encourage, inspire and demonstrate how we can all take the small, everyday, consistent actions necessary to continuously create **WOW**s for each other and our customers on a daily basis.

With this in mind, let's begin our journey together to Turn Your Workplace into a **WOWplace**!

Introduction

WOW!
We say it when we're awed and inspired . . .
We say it when we're amazed and astonished . . .
We say it when we're thrilled and delighted . . .
We say it when we're shocked or startled . . .
We say it with joy – and with sadness . . .

We say it for a million big reasons.

But we also say it for a million small ones – reasons that actually have more impact and meaning over a greater period of time than the big, splashy **WOW**s that have an immediate impact on us, but are usually far too infrequent and short-lived. The small **WOW**s I'm referring to are those of compassion and kindness, empathy and respect – small acts of extreme humanity that add up to big **WOW**s for varying reasons because they are deeply meaningful to the person on the receiving end of them.

When we begin to focus on the small but meaningful **WOW**s we can *consistently* create, rather than focusing solely on the big but fleeting **WOW**s we can *occasionally* create, that's when we realize that *all* of our actions matter, not just *some* of them. This mindset shift enables us to look at the long-term cumulative effect of all our actions, and begin to more consistently behave the way we want to behave and treat others. It is also important to realize that occasional good deeds performed simply to make amends for a rash of bad ones don't quite add up to a **WOW**.

But when we make this mindset shift as an organization, and create a culture that focuses on consistently creating small but meaningful

WOW experiences for everyone around us, that is when we are able to turn our Workplace into a **WOWplace**.

Marking Time

There is a joke circulating the Internet in which a worker says, *"I don't mind coming to work, but that eight-hour wait to go home is a killer!"* Funny joke, but it does hit home because it contains a poignant truth. We are at the point where many associates embark on an eight-hour wait to go home each day – waiting until they can get back to their "real" lives, and to what really matters to them, rather than becoming engaged in the activity at hand in their workplace.

What has happened to cause so many of us to question whether we're really making a difference in our daily lives; whether our jobs and our work have meaning; or if what we do for eight hours a day, five days a week is worthwhile and appreciated? This question is being asked by almost every category and level of associate, many of whom are feeling underappreciated and frustrated by being pitted against their organization's leaders, customers and even each other.

However, as much as we're hearing about disengaged associates and heartless leaders, I believe that we still live in a world where most people *do* care about each other. But "bad" stories make better headlines, so we hear lots of negative hype and not enough positive truth. I also believe that we can help each other and still get ahead in this world. In fact, that's the very thing that often gets other people engaged in helping us succeed. In other words, nice guys and gals don't have to finish last!

These beliefs, as well as four very clear observations, compelled me to write this book:

1. **We could all do with a little more respect in the world.** We must not give in to the temptation to believe that the only way to

combat disrespect from others is by lashing out with disrespect of our own. Especially in the current technological era of being able to say anything (and everything!) electronically and anonymously, without having to come face-to-face with the people we're impacting, we must not forget that there's a real person at the receiving end of our words.

2. **We could all do with a little less fear in the world.** Everyone is afraid of losing their job, losing their power, losing face. As a result, we find it difficult to admit we're wrong, share our knowledge or give credit where applicable.

3. **We could all do with a little more appreciation, recognition and encouragement.** Even though the opportunity for reward or recognition is not what drives most of us to do what's right, it's still nice to have someone notice it occasionally, and take the time to recognize it.

4. **We could all do with a little more inspiration in the world.** Just as we inspire family and friends to feel good about their contributions to the world at large, we must find ways of providing knowledge, coaching and praise to help people succeed and feel good about their contributions in the workplace.

By keeping these observations in mind and committing to doing something about them, we can create more fulfilling workplaces that bring higher success and profit to our companies while instilling hope in our fellow associates that we can make a real difference, no matter what title we hold.

The Multiplying Effect of **WOW** *Experiences*

Why is creating a **WOW** so critical? Why isn't just being good at our jobs enough? If our products are good, or even great, shouldn't that be what matters most?

No. It is *not* enough, because "good" is the bare minimum; it is the baseline. Customers expect both our products and our services to be good. But, in a competitive market, if one or the other (or both) are performing only at the barest minimum level, why would anyone choose to buy from us? Unless we're the only option out there, they won't. Even if we are the only option out there right now, we won't be the only option forever, and it won't take long for potential customers to discover better ones.

But here is the more important point: successfully creating and marketing **WOW** products and services is essential for business success. But it is all wasted effort if we focus solely on the activities that get new customers, without subsequently putting at least as much, if not more, emphasis on actions that keep them.

In reality, it's worse than wasted effort. Effective sales and marketing will eventually work against us by very effectively helping spread negative word-of-mouth much faster than if we had done no marketing or sales at all, as customer after customer who buys from us as a result of these efforts subsequently becomes dissatisfied and leaves. No matter how great our products are, if we do not treat them with respect, customers will not stay with us. In fact, only 14 percent leave because they don't like an organization's products or services; the number one reason customers leave is the way they were treated by an associate.

We have all seen the statistics that reveal the fact that dissatisfied customers will tell many more people about their bad experience than satisfied customers will tell about their good ones. This means that bad news travels at a much higher rate than good news. Therefore, the more people we attract with our **WOW** promises – and subsequently tick off by not living up to that promise – the faster word-of-mouth will negatively impact us, until finally our market "learns" not to buy from us.

The same holds true for associates. We spend so much of our lives at work that it is definitely not worth staying if we're treated disrespectfully by our superiors or colleagues, or if we feel that we're just marking time until we can find something better.

It's time to get back to a "we" mentality (rather than "us versus them"). The only way to do this is to create small daily **WOW**s by focusing on the way we treat each other. By creating **WOW** experiences, we give every associate three things we all desire above almost everything else: being valued, appreciated and listened to.

It's not hard to do, nor does it cost a lot of money. What it boils down to is showing people we care about them. We must never forget how important our small acts of compassion, respect, integrity, and trust are to the people with whom we interact on a daily basis.

It is my intent that this book will provide valuable mindsets, tools, and techniques for creating higher levels of compassion, integrity, respect, and humanity in the workplace, and that improving the way we treat each other on a consistent basis will give each of us the power to turn our ordinary workplace into a **WOWplace**!

> What enables most big **WOW** moments to happen are all the small, consistent **WOW**s leading up to them.

Chapter One:

Setting the Stage

for the **WOW**

[1]

Setting the Stage for the **WOW**

What makes us say **WOW**? Is it incredible athletic ability and accomplishment, such as that of Michael Phelps, the most highly decorated Olympic medalist to date? Maybe it is incredible artistic or musical talent, such as that of Jackie Evancho, the 10-year-old opera singer who burst onto the stage of America's Got Talent in 2010, and recorded a debut album that went platinum when she was only 11. Maybe extraordinary forces of nature like Niagara Falls, or incredible feats of mankind such as fighter planes taking off and landing from aircraft carriers make you say **WOW**.

Two Sides of the **WOW**

All of the above, and more, make us say **WOW**! There are many **WOW**s in big, wondrous, seemingly-impossible events, and in people that move and inspire us and then continue with their lives, as we continue with ours. They are outward manifestations that represent the "fun" side of the **WOW**. But they occur only sporadically, and their effects are fleeting. Let's face it – if these **WOW** moments occurred all the time, they would cease to be **WOW**s because they would then be considered commonplace. So, as wonderful as these **WOW** moments are, we don't live our lives in them every day.

Rather, we live our lives in the more sedate side of the **WOW**, which may look less exciting at first glance, but is absolutely necessary in order for the fun side to exist. This is the side where our pride comes through, and where our dedication, commitment and expertise show us (or *should* show us) that we all matter, and that what we *do* matters, every single day. Everyone who helps create the fun side of the **WOW** knows that the critical factor that allows those moments to happen is what is done leading up to them. It is in the actions taken by the entire team to create small **WOW**s on a daily basis, to be the absolute best they can

> *What allows big* **WOW** *moments to happen are the small, consistent* **WOWs** *leading up to them.*

be and to get the absolute best out of everyone around them. As a result, we must continuously strive to be better, more skilled and more creative in order to produce the next fun **WOW** that will impress an increasingly sophisticated audience.

Ironically, the seemingly sedate side of the **WOW** can actually be more fun, because this is where we get more opportunities to make a difference more often, more consistently, and with more long-lasting effects. How great does it feel to help a customer solve a problem and know that you just made their experience (and their day) a little better? Or to offer someone a few kind words of praise or encouragement that make them feel a little better about themselves? Or to teach someone a new skill or mindset that helps them go on and build a better life? That's where the true **WOW**s are: in helping each other and making our world a better place.

And why do we work hard to create **WOW** products and services? To help others be more successful, make life more comfortable and make needed goods more accessible, convenient and affordable. Of course making money is a crucial part of the equation, but most often it begins with trying to make something better for someone else.

But it takes work. Think about it: Michael Phelps didn't become the most highly decorated Olympic athlete in history without practicing every day for years to become the best he could be. And what would have happened if the people who made the time clock used in one of his crucial races had come to work the day it was manufactured saying, *"I'm tired today. So what if it's off by 1/100th of a second?"* (Phelps came from behind and beat one of his competitors by 1/100th of a second to earn one of his gold medals in 2008.)

A space shuttle doesn't just go to the moon and return safely without an entire team of people striving every day for years to ensure near-perfection at the moment of truth and every step of the way as that feat is accomplished.

And customers and associates are not completely impressed by their experiences with an organization unless all of its people focus on creating **WOW**s; not just on some days, but *every* day.

The Difference Between a Workplace and a WOWplace

What is a **WOWplace**, and how is it different from an ordinary workplace? To reiterate the definitions provided on the first page of this book, here is my definition of each:

Workplace	**WOWplace**
A place where EMPLOYEES HAVE to go because they make a PAYCHECK	A place where PEOPLE LOVE to go because they make a DIFFERENCE

In a workplace, you find employees who are grateful just to have a job . . . any job! They often don't care what it is or how they do it, they're just there for the paycheck.

In a **WOWplace**, you find people (not just nameless, faceless, employees) who are thankful to have *this* job, at *this* company, with *these* people! In a **WOWplace**, people care about delivering **WOW**s to each other, inspiring them to deliver **WOW**s to their customers. Of course, they still care about and need the paycheck, but they also care about doing the job right and find ways to earn their paycheck in a manner that benefit everyone around them, no matter what title or position they hold.

Contrary to popular belief, creating the **WOW** isn't just about big, flashy one-time actions that create fleeting impact and then are gone. Not that those big flashy **WOW**s are not appreciated and needed. After all, they are often what attract people to you – customers and associates alike.

But you also need the small, everyday, consistent **WOW**s that create lasting impact on everyone around you. You need **WOW**s in every single interaction with associates and customers, because *that's* what gets them to stay with you.

Three Components of Creating and Delivering the **WOW**

Creating the **WOW** is not a one-time action. We can't simply create an experience, deliver it once, and consider our job done. It is an ever-improving process for surprising and delighting our customers and each other on a regular basis. We must guard against creating OW experiences for our customers or associates by allowing them to feel that we are taking them for granted, or that they are just another number.

To do this, we focus on three distinct components of creating and delivering the **WOW**:

Creating It: we must find ways to keep moving forward with new **WOW**s, such as offering new products and services, finding new ways in which to offer and deliver them, or discovering ways to improve what we currently offer to keep up with the ever-changing needs and desires of our customers.

Sustaining/Maintaining It: we must find ways to keep it fresh in order to continuously provide the same exceptional experience each and every time, to each and every person with whom we interact.

Improving/Building Upon It: we must constantly create new **WOW** experiences, rather than allowing everything (or anything – even a **WOW**!) to stagnate and go from **WOW** back to ordinary.

*Creating the **WOW***

The first step is creating the **WOW** in the first place. This is where we take a situation that is an OW experience, and find ways to turn it into a **WOW**. It is where we:

- ◉ Identify the current experience and all of its elements.
- ◉ Identify areas for improvement.
- ◉ Brainstorm ideas to provide customers with something new (or something old they've been asking for that we could not – or just did not – provide before, but can now).
- ◉ Analyze the ideas for anticipated impact, feasibility, financial impact, and potential unintended consequences.
- ◉ Develop, train, implement and reward the ideas that can be implemented now, and identify ideas for possible implementation later.

*Sustaining/Maintaining the **WOW***

This step is where we review the **WOW** for processes, procedures, mindsets, and motivation to enable our associates to deliver a consistent experience every time. Through this process, we look for areas where any experience could differ from one occurrence to the next, from location to location or from customer to customer, creating inconsistencies that hurt our brand. It is also the step where we seek ways to breathe new life into repetitive actions to keep them fresh, even when we have done them "a million times."

In order to accomplish this, we have got to make the **WOW** part of our culture, part of everything we say or do. Why are Disney associates called "Cast Members?" It is to help them focus on the fact that they are always "on stage." Imagine going to Disney World, Sea World, or a Broadway show and enjoying the experience so much that you return at a later date to enjoy it again, maybe bringing others with you this time. But instead of the same experience you had on the first trip, the second trip is ho-hum, drab, or even just average, simply because the people delivering the experience have done it 3,753 times before and are just tired of it.

This is not the experience you have anticipated for months! It is not the one you raved about to your friends, who were expecting that same **WOW** experience, only to get something that's "pretty good, but certainly nothing to write home about."

Not only that, but imagine an associate or actor asking you to, *"Please understand that I'm just tired of doing this. Imagine if you had to play the same role over and over again every night for seven years. You wouldn't be able to do it, either!"* Would you understand and say, *"We just paid $10,000 to be here for the week (or $400 to see this show), and it's not what we wanted. But hey, you're tired of it, so that's all right!"* Of course not! No one would expect you to do so, and you would probably want compensation for the disappointment and cost, wouldn't you?

This concept is especially difficult when the **WOW** experience is being delivered to children. How do you ask a child to understand that it was not as good this time because *"Barney is tired (of being Barney!)"* or because *"you've already been here and 'know the drill' so it's not new to you anymore. Therefore, you can just go ahead and I'll be here if you need anything."* All they know is that it is not the same, and they are disappointed.

What seems like "nothing new" to the people providing the experience is perceived very differently by those expecting it.

Service Provider's Perception	Customer's Perception
This is nothing new; you've been here before – you know the drill. Just go ahead and do it again. I'll be around (somewhere) if you need anything.	I don't matter; I'm not special any more. I only mattered the first time I came here. Why are they ignoring me?
Why do I have to go through it all over again the same way, as if it's brand new?	Why aren't I being treated the same way as before? What's changed?
It won't be as much fun because they already know what to expect; it's not new any more.	It's not as much fun as it was the first time; it's not the same.

By not providing the same experience as the first time because it is not new anymore, the service provider actually creates a self-fulfilling prophecy. It is not as much fun – not because it is no longer new to the customer, but because the service provider changed the experience and made the customer feel differently (less special) than they felt the first time around.

Another interesting way to illustrate this point is to think of a favorite song. You know the tune and all the lyrics; you even know the special way that artist sings it. You buy the CD and listen to it until it is figuratively worn out! Years later, the artist goes on a comeback tour to perform his greatest hits. You buy tickets to the concert and eagerly await that "signature" song. But when the artist sings it, he changes it because he is tired of the way he sang it 10 years ago, or because he's thought of a cool new way to sing the song (and assumes his audience will think it's cool, as well).

Bad assumption! Turns out, that is not what you – the fan – wanted to hear! You wanted to hear every nuance of the song you grew up with, the song that was played on your first date, or at your wedding, or when you needed to be re-motivated as you prepared for a 5K run.

The reality is that the artist was focusing so much on what he wanted to do and how he wanted to do it that he lost sight of what his fans really wanted to hear and how they wanted to hear it. But if we want to design and consistently deliver **WOW** experiences, we need to remember that it is not about us. It has to be about them, about what the other person wants, not necessarily what *we* want. It is wonderful when our desires mesh with our customers' desires, and we are all satisfied. But sometimes we just have to "turn that dial" from everyone's favorite radio station: WIIFM (What's In It For Me?) to WIIFY (What's In It For You?), even if it is not exactly our favorite thing or our favorite way.

WIIFY

Improving/Building Upon the **WOW**

This is the final component, which focuses on how we keep improving our services and products to avoid becoming complacent and stagnant, thereby allowing competitors to surge ahead of us. In this step, we find ways to:

- ⊙ Continue filling the current needs of our customers and associates, but do it more effectively, efficiently or profitably.
- ⊙ Build upon existing products and services to fill new needs that arise.
- ⊙ Satisfy new and existing needs in more creative ways, providing better experiences for everyone involved.

By employing brainstorming and other idea-generation methods, including listening to customer complaints and requests to discover where they want us to improve, we cull **WOW** ideas, brainstorm ways to make them a reality, and implement them properly and thoroughly, keeping associates excited and engaged, and customers coming back for more.

Although creating, improving and building upon the **WOW** is not always easy, probably the most difficult component of creating and delivering the **WOW** is sustaining it, being able to consistently create **WOW** experiences for each and every customer, day in and day out – without letting up – because if you let up, you let customers down. In fact, in many industries, inconsistency is one of the biggest drivers of customer dissatisfaction.

If you let up, you let customers down

The same is true with regard to how all associates consistently treat each other. What happens when you never know how someone is going to react to something you have said or done? Will he take offense? Will she get upset or angry over nothing? Will he smile and laugh over a small mistake, forgiving you because he understands that

11

we all make them, or will he rant and rave, humiliate you in public, and possibly even get you fired?

The Vital Importance of Consistency in the **WOWplace**

Consistency is critical to maintaining a **WOWplace** because you can't **WOW** anyone if no one ever knows what to expect from you. The following story aptly demonstrates what happens when people do not know what to expect.

Case in Point:

I was in a store one day, when a woman and her son came down the aisle. The boy stopped in front of a toy that caught his eye and he started asking his mother for it. She said, *"No."* He asked again . . . and again . . . and again. The mother kept denying his request until finally, after about the sixth time he asked, she slapped his backside.

He burst into tears, not from pain but from shock. The woman said, *"What are you crying for? I said 'No',"* to which her son replied, *"Well, how did I know that this time you meant it?"*

Out of the mouth of babes. Apparently, this mother and child had a history of her telling him "no" but changing her mind if he persisted enough. As a result, the child didn't know when he had crossed a line and gone too far. I'm sure many of us can relate.

This is a great example of what happens when people are inconsistent in their words, behavior, or reactions. It does not just apply at home with our children, but everywhere we go, including the workplace. Erratic, inconsistent or unpredictable behavior from leaders creates an atmosphere of distrust that can permeate a workplace and cause associates to be reluctant to proffer creative ideas, either to solve problems or advance innovation. Thus, consistency is imperative, since associates are responsible for delivering the experiences requested and expected by their leaders.

Do You Have Workers, **WOW***ers . . . or OWers?*

Let's face it: we can talk about creating **WOW** experiences all we want, but if all our **WOW** services are not delivered in **WOW** ways, by **WOW** people, with **WOW** attitudes, they are inconsequential. An ordinary workplace will never turn into a **WOWplace** without **WOW** people.

Therefore, we must take inventory: Who is in our organization? Do our associates "bind" customers to us through their words and actions, or do they drive them away through apathy (at best) and disrespect (at worst)? Do we have a workplace with workers and OWers? Or do we have a **WOWplace** with **WOW**ers?

We all know people (inside and outside of the workplace) who are OWers – people around whom we have to "walk on eggshells" because we never know how they will act or react. It is that very randomness and incon-  sistency that cause uncertainty and fear. There is no room in the **WOWplace** for either.

Randomness causes uncertainty and fear

But a **WOWplace** has **WOW**ers – people dedicated to creating the **WOW** at every opportunity, in every interaction. **WOW**ers are people who can be counted on to consistently remain focused on treating others with respect, and as valued human beings – often even when the other party is not behaving respectfully. They keep their eye on the goal, which is to solve a problem, rather than try to disrespect someone else because they have lost control of their emotions, and often their tongue.

What makes someone a **WOW**er? Everyone shows their **WOW** in different ways, and the "test" is not how outgoing someone may or may not be. I have seen many gregarious people give "lip service" to being **WOW**, but cannot be counted on to actually do it. And I've seen many very quiet and shy people who would go to the ends of the earth to help others.

The **WOW** is not in appearances. In fact, how often do we admire someone because of an incredible talent such as acting, singing, or skateboarding, only to find out that the person underneath the incredibly **WOW** surface is not so **WOW** after all? The **WOW** is in people's hearts and their attitude and willingness to go the extra mile to help others succeed. **WOW**ers are people who can be counted on to make others feel safe, valued, respected and engaged. And *that* is accomplished one small **WOW** at a time.

This does not mean **WOW**ers are perfect. They have their moments, just like everyone else. However, because they are much more in control than not, they are more easily forgiven when they behave "out of character" and create an OW rather than a **WOW**.

There are several important factors that make people **WOW**ers, including the fact that:

- ◉ They are secure enough not to be threatened by the WOW actions of others, but recognize and reward those actions, rather than trying to take credit for them.
- ◉ They do not believe that acknowledging others' accomplishments diminishes their own.
- ◉ They never act as though they are too "cool" to be WOWed by – and acknowledge – the actions of others; to laugh or chuckle at a joke, to smile at a kindness or to praise someone for a job well done.
- ◉ They never think they are the only WOWers in the world, but realize that great ideas can come from many sources and are willing to keep an open mind to suggestions from others.

So, how do you develop a process where you can create **WOW**s – and not OWs – *by design*, and not *by mistake*, making it a vibrant and integral component of your culture?

*Creating the **WOW** is a Matter of Will*

Whether you need to go from OW to **WOW**, find ways to consistently keep the **WOW** going, or discover ways to ramp it up in your company, leaders and associates must answer one crucial question: *"To **WOW** or not to **WOW**?"*

This is the question everyone must ask with every interaction with co-workers, bosses or customers. The question every leader must ask is how to inspire their associates to *want* to **WOW**, rather than simply maintaining the status quo or doing just enough to get by . . . maybe. The crucial element to address is that associates will only be motivated to create **WOW**s for others when someone else cares enough to create **WOW**s for *them*.

Creating the **WOW** is a matter of will:

> **W**ill I
>
> **O**r
>
> **W**on't I

"Will I or won't I do what is absolutely necessary to satisfy this customer's needs, or enhance my co-workers' ability to do their job effectively, or even just make someone's day a little more tolerable – and even enjoyable?"

The answer to this one question reveals our willingness and ability to **WOW** everyone around us. Consistently answering this question with "I Will" means the difference between sporadically doing a great job, and regularly doing such an excellent job that it becomes predictable and reliable, and turns into a **WOW** for every customer and colleague we encounter.

Thus, it is important to hire the right people for the position, not only in terms of the hard skills and experience they possess, but for their mindsets and attitudes. Are they flexible? Are they willing to learn and grow? How well do they get along with others? Are they willing to go the extra mile for their customers and their co-workers? Are they a good fit for the position and its responsibilities? Do they possess the emotional maturity and people skills to be successful?

These are not new concepts or questions, but often people are dazzled by hard skills and experience, and assume that the attitudes and mindsets either must be there, or are not so important because the person has already achieved a measure of success.

But if we are trying to create a **WOWplace**, we are not talking about simply achieving a measure of success. We are talking about achieving the highest level of success. Many companies focus on asking prospective associates about their "can do" attitude, when what they *really* should be asking about is their "will do" attitude. *"Can do"* focuses on skills. *"Will do"* focuses on attitude. And attitude is everything.

*Going From OW! To **WOW!***

Everything we collectively do creates either a **WOW** – or an OW – experience for our customers and fellow associates. But what we do after the first **WOW** or the unexpected OW allows us to either **WOW** them by proving what we are made of, or OW them by fulfilling their lowest expectations.

Think of a time when something went wrong with a product or service you had purchased. When you called the company to inform them of the problem, what did you expect them to do? You expected them to fix it, of course! This is only natural. In fact, when you called the company, your Real hope was that they would "make it right" – at *their* cost and *your* convenience – not the other way around.

We expect companies to make things right at their cost and our convenience – not the other way around

But does this always happen? Unfortunately, more often than not the answer is a resounding NO. Newspapers and the Internet are rife with stories of customers having to deal with companies selling products and services that fail to deliver on their promise, cause customers pain or inconvenience, and whose representatives are not empowered to "do the right thing" to "own" and correct the problem. Whether due to ignorance, incompetence or indifference, the actions of these representatives are usually the cause of the biggest OWs and cost companies current business as well as future referrals and repeat business.

In addition to ensuring that associates possess and maintain a *"Will do"* attitude, on the next page is a simple template that will help associates create **WOW**s by design.

*Aim for the **WOW**!*

The template uses a familiar shape to guide your thinking in order to analyze and improve any situation and go from OW to **WOW**. It helps you conduct a gap analysis to determine where disparities exist between the current experience and the desired one.

Imagine that every interaction you have with another person is like a target. Your goal is to **WOW** them, and the **WOW** is the bull's-eye. An OW experience occurs when you miss the target altogether. In between the "OW" and the "**WOW**" are experiences that can be described as "OK" and "Really good." These are the areas where average companies and their associates operate. **WOWplace**s operate

17

in the bull's-eye, with every associate focused on the ultimate goal of creating **WOW**s with every action and interaction.

You will notice that the actions that get you closer to the bull's-eye often start with the knowledge of what creates an OW, as well as building upon the actions that make up the "hits" on the outer rings of the target.

For example, to create a "Really good" experience, we do what is considered "OK" (the bare minimum) and change it or add another action to it. To create a **WOW** experience, we take what was done to create a "Really good" experience and add even more actions to that.

OW!	You missed the mark altogether (didn't even try; didn't make the bare minimum).
OK	You did the bare minimum.
Really good	You're getting closer, but it's not really a **WOW** yet.
WOW!	You've really hit the mark! It's hard to hit it, but well worth it when you do.

To hit the bull's-eye, we must ask ourselves a crucial question for each aspect of the interaction: Will this create a **WOW** or an OW? For example, ask yourself: *Is my goal on the telephone to put a customer in his place because he is treating me badly? Will I allow myself to be* *dragged into a power struggle with this person, lowering my standards and behavior to match his? Is it really about me? Or will I keep my eye on the goal and try to turn that situation around by creating a* **WOW** *for him and a win for me and my company? Is my goal with a co-worker to humiliate her in front of her peers by calling out what she did and chastising her publicly, or is it to help her do her best on the job by coaching and encouraging her in the right direction, privately correcting her on what she could do differently in the future when she makes a mistake?*

Watching For and Performing Gap Analysis Must Become Second-Nature

Rather than being limited to certain situations (after a negative customer event) and certain groups of people involved in the organization (external customers), gap analysis must also occur in the normal course of business. This means that questions are asked:

- Ahead of time, in anticipation of group and individual interactions that have the potential to WOW.
- Every time an interaction between two groups or individuals occurs.
- When positive and negative customer events occur.
- With relation to internal and external customers alike.

To help you make this analysis an easily doable part of your culture, a copy of the full target template, as well as questions to guide your brainstorming as you use it, are contained in the final chapter of this book, **WOW** Tools and Templates. As you go through the book, these concepts will be brought back and applied in each chapter in order to demonstrate and give you practice with how the template may be used in every situation to create **WOW**s for others.

*The **WOW** is Often in the Nuance*

Everything we do contributes to someone's experience. It is in all the little things that don't seem to mean anything separately, but when added together create one big experience. Sometimes it is in something someone says or does; sometimes it is in what they do *not* say or do.

The following stories epitomize the nuances that can help us create **WOW** experiences for everyone around us.

The **WOW** is Not Always in the Answer, But in Ownership of the Situation

> **Case in Point:**
>
> I once had a problem with my bank account and called to find out what happened. The representative didn't know, but offered to check on it and call me back within a day or two.
>
> Late in the afternoon on the second day, she called to inform me that she hadn't gotten an answer yet, but didn't want me to think she'd forgotten about me. She just wanted to ease my mind and tell me she planned to keep trying and hoped to have an answer by the next day. **WOW!**

I was impressed by her actions, even before she had obtained the answer to my original question! In fact, it was likely that I would not be **WOW**ed by the final answer. I would probably be informed of what had happened and how the bank would correct it. No **WOW** there, although the potential for an OW was huge if the bank did not correct the problem quickly.

What **WOW**ed me was the way she handled not just the initial call, but the entire process. She took *ownership* of the situation from beginning to end! She didn't forget about me or pass me off to someone else, then blame *them* when the situation wasn't resolved. She understood that the key to creating a **WOW** experience was in the nuance, realizing that the promise to call back within a day or two, regardless of whether she had an answer or not, was just as important as the answer she would eventually pass along to me.

Most people simply focus on getting the answer, not really paying attention to the experience in the time between the initial call and the final contact. This compels them to create OK (at best) and OW (at worst) experiences for the customer. But if you want to create exceptional experiences for your customers – and for fellow associates as well – remember that the experience starts at the first contact, the first promise, and does not end until there are no more promises to break.

Is Your Phone Greeting a **WOW**?

Case in Point:

The staff at one of my doctors' offices is very friendly, and we talk and joke all the time when I'm there. But on the phone, it is a very different story. When I call, their greeting includes the name of the doctor, but not the name of the person answering the phone. Sometimes I can tell who it is by their voice, but not always. When I give them my name, I am quite surprised (and a little taken aback) to receive stony silence, or a simple *"Hello"* in return. No use of my name (*"Hi, Sandy!"*), and no offer of theirs.

Wait! Are these the same people with whom I constantly joke and laugh while I'm there in person? The difference between their in-person demeanor and their telephone demeanor creates a situation that causes some discomfort when calling their office. It makes me wonder (albeit only for a very short time) if they even remember who I am. And while I feel very valued when I'm in the office, I feel very UN-special when I talk to them on the phone.

This small nuance in communication is exactly the kind of "disconnect" that can cost a business (especially a healthcare-related business, where a personal connection is even more important than in most other types of business) valuable customers.

When someone calls your office, what kind of greeting do they receive? Is it friendly? Informative? Polite, but distant? Does the greeter introduce herself, as well as say the name of the company? And if the caller is well-known to the organization, is she given the warm treatment of someone who is well-known, well-liked, and whose call is valued? Or is she offered the same distant treatment offered to strangers? For that matter, how are strangers treated? Do they feel welcome? Is the person answering the phone smiling, welcoming and enthusiastic, or does she sound tired, bored and annoyed by the call? Are callers given a reason to feel good toward the company, which makes them want to deal with the company further? Or are they given every reason to hang up and find someone who actually welcomes their call – and their business?

On the telephone, all physical cues are absent, so there is no way to make up for a distant tone of voice with a smile or direct eye contact that lets them know you are engaged with them and happy to hear from them. If your tone of voice does not make up for the absence of physical body language cues, you may as well either ignore their call (the equivalent of ignoring them when they are standing in front of your desk) or tell them you do not have time for them right now (or that they are bothering you) – because that is the impression you could be giving with your tone of voice.

Keep in mind that people want three things from other people: to be valued, appreciated and listened to. If you treat someone who feels warmly toward you as if you do not know or recognize them, they will not feel valued. If you make them feel that they are bothering you, they will not feel appreciated. And if you do not enthusiastically respond to what they are telling you, they will not feel listened to.

That adds up to a whole lot of OW – rather than the incredible **WOW** you can create by consistently acting in the same warm, welcoming way whether you are on the phone, in person, or even communicating via e-mail.

Find the Nuances in Your Own Products by Using Them

Case in Point:

I usually go to my bank's drive-up ATM to make deposits and get cash. But I recently found myself near a different branch when I needed to deposit a check. This branch happened to have an outside walk-up ATM, which was convenient and posed no inherent problem.

The *problem* was that sitting right next to the ATM was a trash barrel. First of all, in Florida this can be a smelly proposition, but the problem *that* day was not the smell; it was the fact that it had attracted bees that were flying all around the barrel, as well as the customers trying to use the ATM!

Some people did not notice the bees; others (like myself) were trying to stand as far away from the barrel as possible without losing our place in line. When it was time to approach the ATM to use it, we had to stretch our arms as far as possible to reach the keys, while keeping most of our body away from the barrel.

Although there was plenty of space along the outside wall for bank personnel to place the barrel close enough to the ATM to be convenient for customers, but far enough away to avoid inconvenience caused by smells and insects, apparently no one had taken the time to think it through and find the balance between which factors provided a valued service and which detracted from it. This one small nuance of customer service overshadowed the wonderful services the bank had provided by putting the ATM and the trash barrel out there.

Do you use your own products and services to test them out and see how they work? Do you double-check and at least observe them being used by others to ensure they are the **WOW** you think they are? Not using and observing your own services in action could cause you to overlook vital nuances that can mean the difference between an OK experience and a **WOW**.

You Never Get a Second Chance to Make a <u>Second</u> Impression!

We've all heard the saying that "You never get a second chance to make a first impression." This saying has held up for many years because it's absolutely true. First impressions are important because if we blow that one, we may never get a chance to make a second impression. However, in the world of business, especially in the areas of customer service and its important partner, sales, it is often not about the first impression, it's about the second, a.k.a. the follow-up!

What happens when we do get that all-important chance to make a second impression? Once we have made a great first impression, and someone contacts us to follow up, do we live up to the promise of that first impression? Do we live up to the "elevator speech" we've worked so hard to craft and deliver?

Case in Point:

Many entrepreneurs join leads groups to build relationships and get business leads At one leads group meeting, a lawyer stood up and gave the following "elevator speech" to the group:

"I'm a lawyer, and if you've ever called a lawyer and had them NOT call you back, call me! I'll call you back!"

Fantastic elevator speech! In one sentence, he demonstrated his recognition that one of the biggest problems small business people have with lawyers is trying to get them to return calls. Then he promised to correct that problem if anyone called him. Everyone was very impressed by his personality, message, and promise.

Turns out, a few weeks later I needed some legal advice, so guess who I called? You got it. I called my leads group acquaintance, the lawyer who had made such a great impression on me! How did it turn out?

He never returned my calls!

The truth is that most sales and customer service professionals do not fall down on the first impression. Salespeople go to networking events and put on their "game day" face. They are great at talking to people, getting them interested in what they have to offer. They craft "elevator speeches" and fun, memorable "positioning statements" and then, when they've hooked someone and gotten them interested in doing business with them, they choke! Because the deal isn't sealed right there on the spot, they forget how important the follow-up is.

In customer service, we answer the phone and put on our "game day" voice, politely, cheerfully and respectfully, but if we can't fix their problem immediately on that first call, we also choke! We transfer them, make them repeat their problems and promise calls back, but then never make them, forcing *customers* to call back and start the process over and over again, until it's finally resolved through their diligent efforts (not ours) or they leave. This, once again, goes back to our need to serve customers at *their* convenience and *our* cost, not only in terms of monetary measures, but time and effort.

There are many reasons why these follow-up failures occur:

- ◉ We lose or misplace their contact information and can't call them (sometimes we can't even remember that someone wanted us to call them).
- ◉ We don't have time to call, as day after day after day "gets away from us" because we're overloaded and can't keep up.
- ◉ We pass the information along to a co-worker whom we trust to get back to the person, but they don't do it, and we never follow up to see if it was done.
- ◉ We don't check our e-mail or voicemail for days (or weeks), and let leads go stale and opportunities to serve go past.
- ◉ We get sick and can't get back to them because we're a one-person shop, and we just can't do anything when we get sick.
- ◉ In large call centers, customers often can't call us back personally since the organization is so large. When they do call back,

they have to speak to whomever answers that day, and hope the previous representative made complete notes in the file.

Whatever the reason, does it really matter? Do customers care about our overload, illness, or technological issues? No. In fact, if we can't even take care of them while we're trying to earn their business, they (rightfully) wonder how they'll be treated once we have it! The harm to our reputation and our business caused by falling down on this vitally important **WOW** opportunity is often irreparable.

More importantly, by **WOW**ing potential customers on the first contact, we actually set the stage for (and make an "implied promise" of) just as good an experience on the second one – maybe even better! If that "promise" is broken, the potential customer becomes even more disenchanted than if they'd never established a relationship with us. This makes the fall even harder when it happens, as they feel betrayed or misled: *"I expect that from strangers, but I don't expect it from people I've connected with."*

If you're going to take all the time and effort (and often expense) of trying to make **WOW** impressions on people on your first contact with others, make the most of those opportunities! Put backup plans (and people) in place to take over if you're sick, on vacation, or incapacitated; use technology to help you be more organized and productive; use "tickler" systems to help you remember when to follow up, and with whom; make notes so others can handle the situation if necessary, and so you can remember what's been done. All these little steps add up to one big **WOW** experience!

Make the most of every precious opportunity to connect face-to-face, voice-to-voice and heart-to-heart. Just don't "break their hearts" by forgetting to **WOW** them as much on subsequent contact opportunities as you did on the first one!

Always Do the Right Thing, Even if You Think it Doesn't Matter

Wherever they are, whatever they are doing, **WOW**ers are committed to doing things to the best of their ability, and being the best they can be at that moment. They also commit to doing the right thing, even if they think it doesn't really matter at that moment. They do not make excuses because it's not their company, they are not getting paid enough for the job, or they are just marking time (using the job as a stepping stone) until something better comes along. They realize that if they keep their promises and always do everything to the best of their ability, their commitment will make them stand out, help their organization and create better opportunities more quickly for themselves. Because they feel this way, their beliefs and commitment to doing what's right are very obvious in their consistent actions.

Conversely, if people do not behave in this manner, their beliefs and commitment to doing what's right are not obvious.

Case in Point:

I have belonged to several leads groups. In each group, there were invariably people who talked a good game when it came to getting things done, but never followed through by doing any of it, forcing other group members to pick up the slack.

Those who let their responsibilities slide obviously believed that it didn't matter if they followed through or not in these volunteer positions. In fact, they often justified not doing so because *"I got too busy with my regular job,"* or the belief that *"I don't have to pay as much attention or care to volunteer work as I do in my paid job. In fact, the group is lucky I'm doing it at all!"*

But those who had to do extra work, *on top of their own committed tasks,* didn't feel so lucky. And those with a track record of doing such things didn't get many leads, since few group members felt they could be trusted to keep their word, negating the reason they joined the group: to build relationships and get business.

I have an important question for us all to consider: If the only place I meet or ever see you is in these types of situations, and you do not do the right thing there because you think it doesn't matter, how do I know you will (or can) do the right thing when it does matter?

It always matters! Even if your paid job takes precedence (being a business owner, I am well aware of that reality), if you have made a promise you discover you can't keep, do the right thing by making arrangements for someone else to help you (or do it for you).

Contradictions and Inadvertent Messages

The above situation illustrates a common problem: it is often difficult to recognize the contradictions and inadvertent messages we may be sending with our words or body language. We may never say the words, *"That's not my job,"* but are our actions inadvertently saying them for us?

It is often difficult to recognize the contradictions and inadvertent messages in our own actions.

As illustrated above, there are many ways to find and incorporate the positive nuances in any service situation. If you want to create **WOW**s for customers, take a look at the products and services you provide for them. Then put yourself in their place by using those services (or at least observing them in action) to see where you may be allowing small nuances to undo all the good done by providing them in the first place. Use proactive thinking to envision the way the service will be used and make it the best it can be. Also, become very observant everywhere you go. Examples of the nuances of service are everywhere! Pay attention to them, and then bring them back to your organization to brainstorm how you can apply those lessons there.

Chapter Summary:
How to WOW Through Setting the Stage

1. Two sides of the **WOW.**
2. The difference between a workplace and a **WOWplace.**
3. Three components of creating and delivering the **WOW.**
   a. Creating the **WOW.**
   b. Sustaining/maintaining the **WOW.**
   c. Improving/building upon the **WOW.**
4. The vital importance of consistency in the **WOWplace.**
5. Do you have workers, **WOWers** . . . or OWers?
6. Creating the **WOW** is a matter of will.
7. Going from OW! To **WOW!**
8. Aim for the **WOW!**
9. Watching for and performing gap analysis must become second nature.
10. The **WOW** is often in the nuance.
    a. The **WOW** is not always in the answer, but in ownership of the situation.
    b. Is your phone greeting a **WOW**?
    c. Find the nuances in your own products by using them.
    d. You never get a second chance to make a <u>second</u> impression.
    e. Always do the right thing, even if you think it doesn't matter.
11. Contradictions and inadvertent messages.

Most people don't disengage because *they* don't care. They disengage due to the belief that *others* don't care what they think.

Chapter Two:

Engaging your **WOW**ers

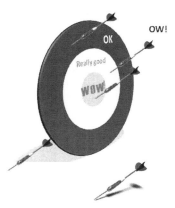

[2]

Engaging Your **WOWers**

According to a 2012 Gallup poll on associate engagement, the ratio of engaged to actively disengaged associates in world-class U.S. organizations, is 9.57 to 1. That is almost 10 engaged workers for every actively disengaged worker. However, in *average* U.S. organizations, the ratio of engaged to actively disengaged associates is 1.83 to 1.* This means that almost half of these workers are disengaged!

This level of disengagement costs U.S. organizations billions of dollars in lost productivity, as well as higher absenteeism, safety incidents, and turnover rates. This is not necessarily because disengaged associates leave, but often because they stay, causing *engaged* workers to leave the company to avoid dealing with them. Therefore, one of a company's biggest concerns is gaining and maintaining a competitive advantage by hiring and retaining engaged workers, and inspiring them to give their best every day.

Competitive advantage comes in many ways. During the Industrial Age (which ended in 1957), it lay in our ability to manufacture superior products. Now, in the Information Age, many experts agree

*Copyright © 2012 Gallup, Inc. All rights reserved. The content is used with permission; however, Gallup retains all rights of republication.

33

that an organization's intellectual assets are one of its biggest sources of competitive advantage. Specifically, competitive advantage lies within the knowledge, innovative ideas, and inspired actions of its associates. Therefore, motivating and inspiring workers to care about the organization's success and contribute to it by engaging and sharing their knowledge and ideas is key.

Explicit vs. Tacit Knowledge

There are two types of knowledge that can be tapped to create competitive advantage: *explicit* knowledge, which represents information that is known and utilized; and *tacit* knowledge, which is the knowledge that exists only in the minds of the current workforce. Many organizations go to great lengths to protect existing known "trade secrets," but not many are going to any lengths to extract the tacit knowledge that represents *potential* trade secrets, process improvements and productivity enhancements that can create **WOW**s for the organization and its customers alike.

For example, front-line associates deal with customers on a regular basis. They know what new and innovative products and services customers desire; they also know what is going wrong – or right – with the company's current products, services, processes, and customer interactions because they are hearing it first-hand every day. Back-office associates who do not deal with customers still use the processes and procedures that support the operation, so they know where improvements can be made to promote efficiency, productivity and profitability. Additionally, many associates are drawn to an organization because they like its products and services. Since they are customers as well as associates, they have a higher level of loyalty and interest in sharing their valuable opinions about what they like and do not like about the products.

The problem is that although these associates have a great deal of knowledge and insight that could help their employer serve customers better, create higher levels of success and help co-workers avoid duplicating their efforts, they are not sharing it. Why not?

Why Don't Associates Share Their Knowledge?

Besides those associates who just don't care or are grappling with emotional factors that cause them to refuse to help others, there are several reasons why *good* associates do not share tacit knowledge:

- The knowledge is too new; they haven't yet had time to tell anyone or note it.
- They don't feel the need to write it down. They may have originally been taught a procedure, but have learned shortcuts, time-savers, money-savers, and new resources to help them along the way. They now perform these shortcuts as a matter of course, so no one else knows about them. If they leave the organization, the shortcuts go with them.
- Fear. Fear of reprisal, embarrassment, failure, job loss; even fear that someone will claim the idea as their own and receive the accolades and any accompanying bonus, promotion or other benefits. Fear is a powerful de-motivator, even in a good economic climate. Add the current economic challenges and it creates a situation where people won't take any chances for fear of paying the ultimate price of losing their job.
- They just don't realize what they have, or that it is of any value. One person may have one piece of a puzzle, a second person may have another, and a third person still another, but no one even knows there's a puzzle! They do not realize what they collectively have because there simply is no forum for the sharing of ideas – good or bad – that would allow anyone to

recognize the formation of a pattern that could provide knowledge to benefit the organization.

⊙ The "no good deed goes unpunished" syndrome, where associates make good suggestions that suddenly become an additional responsibility to implement, manage, and carry to fruition. Sometimes, it even becomes a factor in their performance appraisal, even though it does not come with any promotion or monetary reward.

⊙ But most often, the reason good associates do not share their knowledge and ideas is simply that they are never asked to do so. They may know something that could be of value to the organization, but because there is no forum for sharing, they do not know who to tell, how to tell them, or if anyone would value their opinion. So they remain silent.

Case in Point:

Early in my corporate career, I worked for a company with a women's clothing division. I represented their target demographic: a 25-40-year-old professional woman, and they offered associates a 30 percent discount. Despite these two factors, many of my friends and I repeatedly went to their store and left without buying because we found nothing we liked!

We were aching to tell the company about this and offer viable alternatives to what they were selling. But there was no forum for us to do so; we didn't know who to tell or how to tell them, nor if our opinions would be welcomed or valued. So we kept silent. The kicker is that the corporation employed 10,000 people within a small geographic area, which meant they had access to 10,000 pieces of _free_ market research, if they had only asked their associates two questions: Do you use your associate discount? Why, or why not?

If we had been asked our opinion, we could have helped the company understand that their buyers were missing the mark and we would have felt more valued as associates.

Side Note: This unprofitable division was eventually sold, and then closed its doors.

Case in Point:

During a discussion with a customer service associate, I became extremely frustrated by their complicated process. When I made a suggestion that they look at ways to simplify it, the associate said to me, *"Well, I can tell them, but they won't listen – they never do!"*

Wouldn't you just love to have *that* guy working for you?

The bigger problem in an organization where associate suggestions are ignored or stolen is that associates develop a pervasive culture of hopelessness because they never receive feedback about their suggestions and comments. This results in a feeling of, *"Why bother?"* And when it gets bad enough, they keep their ideas to themselves, but they certainly do not keep their *opinions* to themselves.

Case in Point:

In another recent example, I was working with the Administrative Professionals group of a large company with several different locations in New York. After many years of not providing a forum for Admins to brainstorm together, they began asking their Admin teams to get together, share ideas, and brainstorm ways to help the company.

At one of their very first meetings, the Admins realized they were ordering office supplies from different suppliers; no "official" company supplier had been designated. They decided to contact each supplier and request bids for volume discounts for the entire company. Once they received bids, they selected the best and began ordering all their supplies from that company.

Within the first year, the Admin team saved the company $500,000 in office supplies, eventually adding up to $1 million over time!

It is up to the leaders of the organization to inspire, empower, and enable associates to care enough about their mutual success to share their knowledge before it "walks out the door" and is lost forever, or worse, used by competitors who hire our former associates and use that knowledge to their advantage. On the other side, it is up to associates to take initiative to help whenever and wherever they see opportunities to benefit the organization, its associates and its customers.

*Bringing Out the **WOW***

Everyone has the potential to **WOW**. This potential exists in one of three states in each of us:

Obvious WOW: This state exists in people who have been encouraged and nurtured to **WOW** others. From an early age, they have had champions and cheerleaders who not only encouraged them to create **WOW** experiences for everyone around them, but also gave them the tools necessary to think and act in a way that accomplishes this goal.

*__What to do for them:__ Continue to encourage and reward them for creating the **WOW**. Do not stifle their creativity or punish them for taking reasonable risks to achieve stretch goals (goals that they have to "stretch" for in order to achieve).*

Potential WOW: This state exists in people who have been encouraged to use their talents to **WOW**, but have had no role models to emulate, so they have never been taught how to do it. They desire it fiercely, but just don't know what to do, or even how to begin. In this case, the absence of obvious **WOW** is merely due to their lack of knowledge on how to demonstrate it.

__What to do for them:__ Give them encouragement, tools and training to teach them how to create the WOW; then reward them when they take the risk to do so.

Buried WOW: This unfortunate state exists in those who have had their hearts and minds stomped on. As a result, they have learned to bury those instincts out of self-defense, loss of self-confidence and self-esteem, and feelings of hopelessness. They need someone to express faith that they have **WOW** potential, set higher expectations of them, and give them a chance to fulfill those expectations, thus proving to themselves and to others that the **WOW** really is there.

> ***What to do for them:*** *Lead by example; show them what happens when you create WOW experiences for others. Give them proof that it can be done and that it does work, and provide encouragement, training, and time to overcome these experiences to create the WOW.*

Clearly, it is crucial to our own vitality, health and fulfillment to keep ourselves in a state of Obvious **WOW** because this is where we are able to do the most good for ourselves and others.

*Ideas for Engaging Your **WOWers***

How do we remain inspired to do our best every day, where we live and work? What can we do to create a work environment that inspires everyone to be fully engaged so they can – and do – give their very best? One of the best ways to engage people is to show them that we are fully engaged ourselves. As a part of the team, we must be willing to do ourselves what we are asking them to do. That is not to say that we have to do every aspect of every job every day; this is why others are hired to help us. But it *does* mean that we do not refuse to help out in any capacity when needed. If leaders do not want to hear, *"That's not my job!"* from associates' lips, associates must not hear it from their leaders' lips, either.

Another way to engage workers is to let them know that they make a difference, and that their work, opinions and ideas matter, regardless of their position in the organization. Most associates do not disengage because *they* don't care. Associates often disengage due to their belief that *no one* cares what they think. It is amazing how many people will engage/re-engage when they believe their opinion matters, and when they receive even the smallest rewards for their efforts. This does not always entail monetary compensation, but includes recognition and encouragement, as well as coaching and promotion.

Here are some actions that have worked for many companies:

Listen to your associates. Give them a forum for sharing and suggesting new ideas; not the traditional locked suggestion box that invites only lewd suggestions and meaningless complaints. Create a face-to-face forum – or at least a non-anonymous forum – where great ideas can be proffered, tips shared, suggestions made, resources brought to light – anything that is meaningful and can help the organization move forward in terms of productivity, efficiency, profitability and associate and customer experiences. Be careful not to perpetuate the "no good deed goes unpunished" syndrome by overburdening associates with the responsibility for implementing good ideas alone. Assign teams, ask for volunteers, and offer help as well as celebrations, rewards and incentives for participating in the project and producing results.

Pre-reward the behavior you wish to see in others. Coach others on how to accomplish their assigned tasks. Associates often fall short of their goals because they either are not clear on what the goal really is, they don't know how to accomplish it, they do not have the tools to enable them to succeed, or they have been de-motivated along the way by the feeling that what they do doesn't matter anyway, so "why bother?" If someone shows a willingness to accomplish the goals you set forward, show them how to do it and reward and encourage them, even if they have not gotten it 100 percent right just yet. Show them where they are doing well, and coach them to get to the next step.

Model the behavior you wish to see in others. No one will behave in the desired manner if they observe others demonstrating different behavior and getting away with it. The old adage, *"Do as I say, not as I do"* will never fly in the **WOWplace**. No one can be above the rules, no matter what level or position they hold. Even if you do not publicly chastise others (which is understandable, as this is actually not desirable at any level), the organization must be confident that there is fairness in the workplace, and that associates at the upper levels are being held to the same standards as those expected from associates at the lower levels.

Case in Point:

Just prior to beginning my term as Chairman of a volunteer group, I was told by the outgoing leader that the Admin who worked for the group wasn't able to perform the duties required of her, and that I would have to fire her. Great way to start my term!

I decided to wait before taking any action and see for myself where we might be able to work things out, and told her that I would be looking for her to "cover my back" regarding organizational policies, procedures, etc., because she had more experience at that organization.

What I discovered was that while she did lack certain Admin experience, she possessed both organizational knowledge and a desire to serve. So, if she completed even a portion of a given assignment correctly, I told her how much I appreciated what she had done, and then coached her on what the next step could be, as well as how she could think proactively about all necessary steps the next time a similar situation arose.

By pre-rewarding her for the next step in the process, it helped her begin to foresee those next steps on future projects and perform them without further coaching. She actually became my biggest asset as a result, and the need to fire her was eliminated.

Tie rewards to performance. No organization can afford to waste time and resources on nice ideas where beehives of activity occur, but no results are produced; and no engaged associate feels good about being part of a team that is not generating success. Be sure associates know how to earn the rewards, what tools are available to help them, and when and how rewards will be given. Remember that success begets success. When associates know success is measured, celebrated and rewarded, it makes them feel proud to be part of a winning team, and inspires them to create even more success.

Recognize and tap into associates' hidden and under-utilized talents. No one uses every single talent and ability they possess in any position, no matter how challenging. There are always hidden or under-utilized talents that could be of use in new situations, inside and outside the workplace. By recognizing a co-worker's hidden talents, you may be able to use their skills in that area to create higher success for them and the entire organization.

Case in Point:

In the early 1980s, I worked for the Sr. VP of MIS (Management Information Systems, which is now called IT) at one company. Word processing and personal computers were just coming onto the scene, and I was fascinated by it all. One day, I blurted out to my boss that I *"loved all this computer stuff!"*

When a new word processing package crossed his desk a couple of weeks later, he remembered my comment and asked me to try out the product, see if I could get it to work, and let him know what I thought of it. I tried it and got it to work, but didn't like it much. I typed up a report and gave it to him for his review.

About three weeks after submitting my comments to my boss, a review of that product was published in a computer magazine, and it mirrored the same observations I had just put in my report to my boss! Upon comparing my comments to the review, he immediately had me join a company-wide project team tasked with bringing word processing into the organization. I was thrilled with his confidence in me, his recognition of a talent I didn't know I had, and the opportunity to learn new skills.

Get executives on the front lines once in a while. Keep them more connected to the customer experience so they can see first-hand how it works and where it could be improved.

Have associates from highly successful locations share their success strategies. If things are going great in one location, tap into the tacit knowledge of the workers at those locations. Their ideas can be shared to help other locations create **WOW** experiences, too. This will show them you respect and appreciate them, get them engaged in helping the company and fellow associates, and boost their self-esteem.

Chapter Summary:
How to WOW Through Engaging Your WOWers

1. Explicit vs. tacit knowledge.
2. Why don't associates share their knowledge?
3. Bringing out the **WOW**.
   a. Obvious **WOW**.
   b. Potential **WOW**.
   c. Buried **WOW**.
4. Ideas for engaging your **WOW**ers.
   a. Listen to your associates.
   b. Pre-reward the behavior you wish to see in others.
   c. Model the behavior you wished to see in others.
   d. Tie rewards to performance.
   e. Recognize and tap into associates' hidden and under-utilized talents.
   f. Get executives on the front lines once in a while.
   g. Have associates from highly successful locations share their success strategies.

The **WOWplace** Rules

Rules

Rules for Engagement

*Higher engagement for everyone in the **WOWplace***

Chapter Three:

WOWplace Rule #1

A WOWplace is Safe

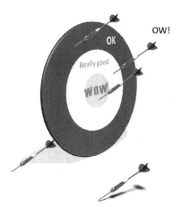

A **WOWplace** is Safe

I f we intend to leverage the power of our associates' innovative thinking and ideas, we must encourage them to take reasonable and appropriate risks to serve customers and each other in an effort to help the organization succeed. To do this, associates must feel safe in taking the necessary risks to create **WOW** experiences.

It is important to keep in mind, however, that what constitutes a risk for one person – or for those at one level of an organization – does not constitute a risk for another. For some, risk involves investment of company funds or implementing new ideas. For others, it is a risk just to apply their own judgment in any given situation.

Case in Point:

I was in California for a luncheon keynote and had just completed the technical rehearsal, when I decided to quickly visit the restroom and return to the ballroom for the keynote. While I was out of the ballroom, ticket-takers had been stationed at all the doors, as this was a specially-ticketed event.

I started to go back into the ballroom, when a ticket-taker put her hand out and said, *"I'm sorry, you can't go in without a ticket."* I thought she was kidding. I looked up at the poster of me that was positioned next to the door and said, *"That's pretty funny!"*

I tried again, but she again stopped me. Even after directing her attention to the poster beside her that contained my picture and telling her I was the speaker, she would not let me in. I had to find the conference organizer, who assured her it was OK to let me in!

I am sure we can all imagine the training she must have received that morning: *"This is a specially-ticketed event. Don't let anyone in without a ticket."* Obviously, she considered it too high-risk to use her judgment and let *anyone* in without a ticket, including the speaker, so she turned her common sense to the "off" position and refused to let me pass!

Whatever their situation, the above example demonstrates the fact that we must help our associates decide which type of situation they are working in at any given time; either one in which their judgment is desired and needed, or one where they must follow procedures almost without question, and that they feel safe in making that judgment call.

Trying to Succeed . . . or Simply Trying Not to Fail?

In order to encourage people to share information, collaborate and create **WOW** experiences for each other and for customers, leaders must set the tone. It comes from the top down, and there can be no disconnect in the middle management layer, since this is the layer that interacts most with the rest of the associates. So, the question is, what tone are we setting? We must make our organization safe! In other words, are our associates trying to succeed, or are they simply trying not to fail?

There is a big difference! One mindset focuses on possibilities and success, the other on fear and failure. What do we say and hear if we are trying to succeed? We hear statement such as, *"I have to try that. I can't afford not to try that!"* But, when our workers are just trying their hardest not to fail, we hear things like, *"I can't afford to try that. What if I fail? I can't take that risk!"*

Case in Point:

I once read a story of a CEO who had an Executive Team member who made a mistake – a big one – that cost the company two million dollars! When the executive who made the mistake was called into the CEO's office, he said, *"I guess you're going to fire me, huh?"* The CEO replied, *"Are you kidding? We just invested $2M in your training. You're not going anywhere!"*

This was a huge **WOW** on the part of the CEO. Not only did this exceptional leader give his executive the leeway to try for a stretch goal, but when he did not reach it (and in fact, it went the opposite way), he didn't make him pay the ultimate price by firing him. As a result, how committed do you think the executive will be when trying to make up for that mistake? My guess is, very!

People will make mistakes. There is no question about it. But they still have to feel safe enough to try to do reasonable things without the fear of having to pay the ultimate price for taking reasonable actions while trying for a stretch goal. Do your people feel safe to try to create **WOW**s? The issue is even more critical to examine, especially in the difficult economy we are currently experiencing. Many people have spouses who have already lost their jobs. Most of them, understandably, will not take any risks with their jobs. And if they do not feel secure enough to try new and exciting actions, they won't. They will hunker down and do the same-old, same-old until you either fire them, lay them off or go out of business yourself because you have done nothing exceptional, and have not allowed your *associates* to do anything exceptional to prevent that from happening. Only exceptional organizations pull through difficult times. When they do, they actually do not just survive . . . they thrive!

How do you know if your environment is safe? Ask yourself the following questions:

- What is our company's position on creativity, innovation and risk?
- Do I know the company's position? Can I clearly articulate it to others?
- How comfortable am I taking risks in my company?
- What will happen if I try and fail?
- How do we treat people who take risks – even sound ones – for the good of the company?
- What are the consequences? Expectations?

If you don't know the answers to these questions, associates won't know them, either. And if they don't know, they won't try! This is especially true in an economy where, if they lose their job, it may be a long time before they can find another one. Those in upper-level positions may have forgotten how intimidataing it can be to share an idea and risk public humiliation or retribution by a boss or vin-

If you don't know, associates won't know . . . and if they don't know, they won't try.

OW!

dictive co-worker who may view new ideas as criticisms or threats. We can never forget how it feels to be afraid for your job as a consequence of not following the rules "to the letter," even to the detriment of the ultimate goal of those rules.

How Are Your Service Recovery Policies?

One way to help associates use their judgment and help serve customers better is through Service Recovery. Service Recovery refers to the policies put in place to help alleviate a customer service situation where something has not gone as intended for the customer. The policies are put in place to help both the organization and the customer "recover" from the incident.

Obviously, this can be a difficult proposition for both the associate and the organization. Therefore, it is important to set guidelines so associates can make the right choices. Let them know what their limits are, and what circumstances allow them to use their judgment in fixing an OW situation. By doing this, we empower associates to "do the right thing" for the customer, at least to a reasonable extent, without having to call in a supervisor or manager to do so, basically enabling the supervisor or manager to create the **WOW** experience while the associate stands helplessly by, feeling powerless to even do their job properly.

The Anatomy of the **WOW**

In fact, let's put ourselves in the shoes of associates who are tasked with delivering the **WOW**. What do they experience every step of the way? How do we ensure that every person involved in delivering the **WOW** – from the associate, to the manager or supervisor, to the customer, to the organization at large – gets to do so, and experiences the benefits of delivering that **WOW** experience?

I have developed another model called *"The Anatomy of the WOW,"* which allows us to analyze every touchpoint (point of contact with another person) from the viewpoint of everyone involved in the entire transaction. This helps us create **WOW**s for everyone involved, for the company as a whole, and not just the customer or associate directly involved in the actual interaction. The following story illustrates how this tool is used, and why it is important to perform this type of analysis for all those who are expected to deliver the **WOW**.

Case in Point:

A friend of mine once worked in the pro shop of a golf club that also had resort villas and a golf school. A couple rented a villa, signed up for golf lessons and planned to play golf there for a week. On the first morning of lessons, resort staff picked up the couple's golf bags and delivered them to the golf course for their lessons. The man's bag made it to the course, but the woman's bag got lost in transit.

Associates had the authority to lend her a set of clubs and a bag to use for her lessons until her bag could be found. However, her golf glove was in her lost bag, and associates did not have the authority to give or lend her another one. They quickly looked around for a manager or supervisor to authorize this, but one could not be found. This left her with two choices: either buy a new glove for $60, or take her chances without one and hope she didn't get blisters. She opted to avoid needlessly buying an expensive glove, and golfed without one, hoping they would find her bag soon. Predictably, she got a blister and was forced to buy a glove at that time.

The next day, when a manager was told what had happened, he offered his deepest apologies to the customer and refunded her money. However, by that time, the damage was done, literally and figuratively.

Let's look at what happened from the viewpoint of all parties:

⊙ A mistake was made (OW for everyone involved).

- Although service recovery policies were in place to lend her some clubs and a bag, no policy allowed front-line associates to give or lend her a glove (a small positive for the clubs, an OW for the glove).

- The woman got a blister and had to buy a glove (two big OWs for everyone).

- The couple most likely spread the word to other people with whom they had contact that afternoon and evening (OW for the company).

- The next day, the manager apologized and refunded her money (a small positive for him as he swooped in and "saved the day" and a small comfort for the customer, but still an OW for the associate who could do nothing positive to help his guest).

The Need for Service Recovery

Service Recovery Policies are established to guide associate actions and help organizations recover from the unfortunate incidents that inevitably occur when a service situation goes wrong. These policies focus on what associates can do to correct the problem. At their discretion, associates may also give customers small "peace offerings" to appease customers if a situation is severe enough.

If a service recovery policy had been in place that allowed an associate to use his own judgment within guidelines – perhaps a fixed amount of money up to $100 (considering this couple was spending thousands of dollars at the resort that week) – he could have created an instant **WOW** and felt great about his job and his actions by giving the woman everything she needed to prevent her from experiencing even one moment of consternation due to their mistake.

What was a **WOW** turns into, "Well, it's the least they could do!"

Although the situation was eventually corrected, it became a case of *"Well, it was the least they could do!"* instead of reaching its true **WOW** potential.

Do your service recovery policies help people use their good judgment (within set guidelines) to help them create a **WOW** for your customers? Or do they unnecessarily tie associates' hands, leaving them feeling as frustrated and helpless as the customers they are attempting to **WOW**?

The template entitled *Anatomy of the WOW* shown on the next page illustrates each step of this scenario, and the effect on each party involved. Use the blank template in the **WOW** Tools and Templates chapter to analyze the anatomy of each touchpoint of each experience in your organization, and figure out how to ensure that everyone feels valued – and valuable – every step of the way.

Anatomy of the WOW

Event/Event Phase	WOW Impact: Customer Experience	WOW Impact: Associate Experience	WOW Impact: Supervsor/ Manager Experience	WOW Impact: Company Experience/ Rep.
A mistake is made	Negative	Negative	Neutral	Negative
A small, logical action was taken to correct it	Positive	Positive	Neutral	Positive
Another problem anticipated	Negative	Negative	Neutral	Negative
Associate not empowered to fix new problem before it happens. Customer forced to choose between two bad *solutions* (lesser of two evils)	Doubly Negative	Doubly Negative	Neutral	Doubly Negative
New problem inevitably occurs	Doubly Negative	Doubly Negative	Neutral	Doubly Negative
No supervisor/ manager available to fix it	Doubly Negative	Doubly Negative	Neutral	Doubly Negative
Supervisor/ manager available, but too late	Doubly Negative	Doubly Negative	Negative	Doubly Negative
Time lapses between problem and cure	Doubly Negative	Doubly Negative	Neutral	Doubly Negative
Supervisor/ manager available and fixes the problem	Positive	Neutral	Positive	Positive (maybe)

Where is the **WOW** for anyone? Especially for the associate? There are hardly any positive impacts on the associate in this situation!

The Need for Service Recovery Recovery

Unfortunately, the Service Recovery phase of the transaction often breaks down to such a degree that customers and associates must subsequently recover from the Service Recovery phase, creating a need for a Service Recovery Recovery phase (a.k.a., calling in a supervisor or manager to smooth the ruffled feathers of all parties).

Let's look at the reasons behind the ever-growing need for Service Recovery Recovery. Service Recovery measures normally come into play only after a customer service "incident" has occurred. And although I am sure we can all think of a few notable exceptions, the current norm during these interactions is that a prescribed response is delivered by bored, upset or disengaged associates who have no authority to veer from the prescribed action or script, even the least little bit, and therefore have no opportunity to truly **WOW** customers. They are limited to merely trying to appease or "handle" them as quickly and cost-effectively as possible. Thus, they are not able to deliver what is really needed until the customer becomes so agitated that the supervisor must come in and "save the day" by offering measures the associate should have been empowered to offer before it reached that point.

If the customer service associate is in a call center, it is even more challenging, since these associates usually just read the prescribed response to the customer for several reasons:

- ⦿ They are too new, un-trained, un-practiced and un-polished to engage in a substantive dialogue with the customer, rather than reciting a canned monologue at the customer.

- ⦿ They do not care enough about the company, the policies or the customer to learn what the policies mean or how they can help the customer and the company.

- They do not speak the customer's language fluently enough to rely on their conversational skills without the script.

- They throw in obligatory "personalization" words (such as inserting the customer's name) at set intervals, regardless of whether they naturally fit or flow in the conversation.

- They are pressured to meet quotas, with their calls timed to prevent them from spending too much time with any one customer, and subsequently being punished for doing so, even when necessary.

If we continue these practices, or continue to withhold the "good stuff" until a customer is really aggravated, it lessens the impact of any peace offering, because the customer is even more angry and frustrated and must now be appeased at a higher level. At some point, the **WOW** becomes impossible when the level of appeasement needed to mitigate the situation becomes prohibitively high.

The Need for Service PREcovery

But what if we are able to exceed customer expectations? What if we are able to plan to succeed at accomplishing much more than the lowest expectation of simply "handling" situations or "appeasing" upset customers when things go wrong? What if we set out to show them what we are really made of, and **WOW** them, causing everyone to emerge unscathed, and even ecstatic, over a pleasantly unexpected turn of events?

What if policies were established to actually **WOW** customers on a regular basis, regardless of whether or not something has gone wrong, either to prevent anything from going wrong or to **WOW** customers, simply because we care that much about them and their experiences with us?

What if we could also apply those same principles to our interactions with fellow associates, either to prevent things from going wrong, or to **WOW** each other, simply because we care about each other and the quality of our daily experiences together?

What if we created Service PREcovery policies – actions intended to help associates think proactively and far enough ahead to create a **WOW** and prevent further complications during the Service Recovery phase, or prevent causing any complications at all during our initial interactions with customers and each other? What if associates were trained to think ahead to any possible complications that might occur and prevent any unfortunate occurrences from happening at all?

An impossible dream? I don't believe so. It may be impossible to prevent all unfortunate incidents from occurring, but proactive thinking and action by associates can prevent some of them from happening, and that is an improvement over what normally happens now: no proactive thinking and no forethought of the possible ramifications of our actions and words, resulting in a breakdown of trust, compassion and respect on the part of both parties.

Procedure-Based Work vs. Goal-Based Work

I have a fairly extensive background in Information Technology, so I am going to borrow a set of terms from IT and apply them to knowledge-based strategy. In this application, we create two categories of knowledge work: procedure-based work and goal-based work.

In procedure-based work, the focus is obviously on the procedure for performing an action. This scenario is more rigid because deviations from the procedure could result in product defects, missed steps in critical processes, or even injury and/or loss of life. Therefore, the procedure must be followed to the letter.

With goal-based work, the focus is on the goal to be achieved by the action being taken; it is much more flexible and actually demands individual judgment in order to accomplish the goal and create the highest level of satisfaction and service.

Whenever we ask people to perform a task, we must let them know whether it is a situation in which they are to "follow the procedure" or use their judgment and be more flexible in order to accomplish the intended goal. Each is appropriate in different situations, and each requires different motivation, tools and execution in order to be successfully accomplished.

It is an unnecessary risk on the part of both management and associates to use judgment in the absence of clear guidelines. But if the right people are in the right position, and they are given clear guidelines to follow that are flexible enough to allow them to create **WOW** experiences, but keep them from doing harm to themselves, customers or the organization, **WOW**s can happen more often than we think.

The associate who denied my entrance into the ballroom to deliver my speech was so focused on the procedure that she lost sight of the goal, which was to prevent people from sneaking in without paying and getting the lunch, the book, and the speech, not to prevent the speaker from delivering it! And the example of the golf associate who could not offer a customer a glove knew the right thing to do, but was not empowered to do it. Both of these goal-based scenarios could be fixed with the right associates, given the right training and mindsets, and armed with the right tools to deliver the **WOW** experience they should deliver. But this takes trust on the part of both employers and associates.

*Trust in the **WOWplace***

No one enjoys entering situations where trust is lacking. They will enter if they must, but they do not enjoy the experience and, once there, can't wait to leave. A **WOWplace** simply cannot exist without trust, which is a two-way street:

- One party must be trusting.
- One party must be trustworthy.

Most of us have a sincere desire to both trust and be trusted; we want to prove our trustworthiness in any given situation. It is usually only when trust is broken that people become disenchanted and disengaged and stop caring whether or not they keep their own promises.

Think of how much trust your boss places in you by hiring you. If you are a supervisor or manager, think also of how much trust you must place in the people you hire. Every boss is aware of the need to trust associates to keep the promises they make in their job interview.

We all make promises in the workplace. As hired associates, we promise to:

- Do our job to the best of our ability.
- Help the company achieve its goals.
- Support and encourage co-workers by being a team player.

As employers in the position of hiring others, we promise to:

- Treat those we hire with respect.
- Pay them what we promised, in the timeframe promised.
- Provide benefits and tools to help them succeed.
- Care about them as individuals, as well as associates.

Few things help an individual more than to place responsibility upon them and let them know that you trust them.

Keeping Our Promises as Leaders

We make many promises as organizational leaders, from explicit promises to follow our stated values to implicit promises, such as treating associates right, paying them fairly and providing opportunities for them to learn and grow as they work to help the organization succeed. Promises must be conducted on a two-way street. Associates promise to help the organization and organizational leaders in return, promise to treat associates well.

As a result, maintaining trust means keeping those promises, which is done in many ways. One of the most difficult often comes back to modeling the behavior we wish to see in others. We cannot, as leaders, lose control, belittle others, talk behind people's backs, or display a myriad of other behaviors that appear to be "excused" because of the level we have reached in the organization. Too often in ordinary workplaces, we hear of associates who are de-motivated by the fact that the rules seem to be different for the organization's leaders than they are for the followers.

While leaders cannot (and should not) publicly explain every single detail of what goes on in those positions, it is imperative that they communicate the fact that while decision-making and levels of authority differ at different levels, the rules of basic human conduct do not. These rules and the concepts behind them must be the same for everyone at every level, and this fact must be clearly communicated and demonstrated.

For example, in the situation of the executive who made a $2 million error, he was not fired because he had not overstepped the bounds of his authority, but had simply made a mistake. We would never expect an entry-level associate to make a $2 million mistake because that would probably mean he had overstepped the bounds of his authority. But if an entry-level associate *did* make a mistake without overstepping his authority, especially when trying to reach a stretch goal to help the organization, he should not be fired. While the level of authority and its resultant cost is different for each of these people, the underlying concept is the same.

Sometimes the problem is that associates at lower levels do not know if an executive has paid a consequence for misbehavior because those consequences are normally not done in public nor made public knowledge. Associates should be asked to respect the privacy of the individual (just as they would want their privacy respected if they were being chastised) and not look for specific details, but to somehow be reassured that the rules apply to all. What that looks like specifically will vary from one organization to another, but the concepts must be proven. If mistrust has been a part of a particular organization, it may take time for associates to trust that the rules are being followed fairly. Over time it will become clear how an organization operates, and trust can be re-established by making and enforcing the rules fairly, and by leaders personally demonstrating the behaviors they wish to see in others.

Keeping our promises usually means also providing associates with personal development opportunities, as well as a career path within the organization. In fact, according to recent surveys, the number one characteristic that attracts people to a particular workplace is the opportunity to develop a career path. Many companies focus on ensuring the associate is successful in the position for which they were hired. But associates want at least the opportunity to be successful in all positions with the company, not just the initial one. How often do we see and hear horror stories of people who are promoted to higher positions because they demonstrate superior technical skills in their current position, but fail miserably after being promoted because they do not possess the soft skills necessary to succeed in that new position? Therefore, if we want to hire from within (as many companies find beneficial) and help associates succeed within their promised career path, we must better prepare them for leadership positions beyond their current position before they receive the promotion.

Even if your organization is too small to help associates achieve a higher position there, you can still help them develop and prepare for a higher position elsewhere. We all know that most associates will not be with us for life, but this does not mean we shouldn't help prepare them for success later in life by failing to offer exceptional training and coaching now. For example, I will never forget the opportunities provided to me by the manager I previously mentioned who put me on the company-wide project to select a word processing package for our company. That opportunity led to my ability to learn and become extremely comfortable with technology, subsequently become a systems analyst, start my own desktop publishing company, and at age 56, receive a Masters degree in Information Management Systems! Even though I did not stay at that company forever, I gave my all while I was there and am forever grateful to my manager for recognizing and giving me a chance to utilize my talents in new directions.

IDP's (Individual Development Plans) that identify, promote and measure career objectives and development of personal and interpersonal skills, attitudes and aptitudes are another value-added benefit that should be created for associates at all levels. Company-paid training and tuition reimbursement also helps them progress in the desired direction.

Whether or not the company offers training or pays for outside training in the area of personal development (communication, leadership skills, team-building, etc.), associates at all levels should seek this training on their own. Not only will this prepare them for progressively higher positions and added value for any company, but it also reveals what they are made of when they take the initiative to obtain higher levels of training and development on their own. If an organization can see that an associate is willing to go to greater lengths than the average associate to improve their knowledge or skills, they will stand a better chance of getting the organization to open up new opportunities for further learning and growth.

Case in Point:

When my husband, Bruce, was in the military (years ago), he found out that some of the people in his outfit were going to attend a computer programming course that he also wanted to attend, as he had ambitions to become a programmer. Unfortunately, he was not in the proper division to receive this training and was told he could not attend because they could not afford to pay for anyone else.

Undaunted, Bruce told his superior officer that he wanted to go so badly that he would pay for the training himself; all they had to do was to let him attend. His superior officer was so impressed that Bruce would do this that he said, *"If he wants to go so badly that he'll pay his own way, we want him."* Not only did he allow Bruce to attend the training, but Bruce did not have to pay for it.

Just by taking the initiative to go for something himself, regardless of whether or not his employer provided it, Bruce showed them what he was made of!

One more important point to remember is that if leaders allow associates to stagnate, either in their training, skills or attitudes, they inadvertently do a great disservice to the organization and their associates. When associates are not expected to move forward, they often become complacent, risk-averse and resentful when asked to learn new skills. This not only holds the company back, but if that associate ever wanted – or needed – to change jobs, they would not be an attractive option in a highly competitive job market because their skills would be outdated and inadequate for any job in a progressive company. Therefore, one of the best things we can do as leaders is to help associates keep their skills and attitudes at their most professional and competitive level.

Case in Point:

At one of my client companies, a new piece of software was brought into the company to help customer service representatives handle more customers more efficiently. Some long-time associates resisted learning it, balking at the change and at being forced to learn new technology. At the same time, a new associate who already knew the software was hired into the department. She was immediately able to handle five times the workload of current associates, a startling demonstration of the value of keeping up with new software.

Not only did this demonstrate that associates are much more valuable if they keep their skills up to date, but it also demonstrated the favor the company was performing by offering associates *paid* training to keep their skills up to date and make them more valuable associates, not only there, but at any company to which they might apply in the future.

Organizational Justice and Its Role in Motivating Associates

In order to better understand how to motivate associates, it is beneficial to have at least a passing understanding of the concepts of organizational justice at work in a group environment. There are three types of organizational justice that affect associate perceptions of fairness and justice in the workplace:

1. **Procedural Justice,** which is defined as "fairness regarding procedures." It refers to whether or not associates are given a chance to offer input into the design and implementation of organizational systems.

2. **Interpersonal Justice,** which refers to how associates are treated by an authority figure, such as a supervisor or manager,

especially when receiving performance feedback by that manager.

3. **Informational Justice,** which refers to the quality of explanations given by a manager or supervisor about a process, procedure or policy.

Research shows that all three types of justice have strong implications for desired associate outcomes such as trust, commitment and job satisfaction, as well as undesirable outcomes such as withdrawal. Associates have a much higher perception of fair treatment in the workplace when higher levels of interpersonal justice (where treatment by managers is respectful and preserves the associate's dignity) and informational justice (with thorough explanations offered for the use of complex or new policies, as well as during feedback sessions such as performance reviews) are present. The big ah-ha was that the presence of informational justice more positively influences associate trust in the manager than the presence of interpersonal justice and procedural justice. This demonstrates associates' strong desire for clear explanations and direction from their leaders over other types of "fairness factors" in the workplace.

Chapter Summary:
How to WOW Through Making the WOWplace Safe

1. Determine if your associates are trying to succeed . . . or simply trying not to fail.
2. Examine your service recovery policies.
3. The Anatomy of the **WOW**.
4. The need for Service Recovery.
5. The need for Service Recovery *Recovery*.
6. The need for Service PREcovery.
7. Procedure-based work versus goal-based work. Does everyone know the difference and when to use which?
8. There are two parts to trust in the **WOWplace**: one party must be trusting; the other must be trustworthy.
9. Keeping our promises as leaders.
10. Organizational justice and its role in motivating associates.
    a. Procedural Justice.
    b. Interpersonal Justice.
    c. Informational Justice.

Chapter Four:

WOWplace Rule #2

A **WOWplace** is Respectful

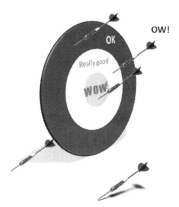

A **WOWplace** is Respectful

What causes a workplace – or any place – to become an environment where people really want to be an integral part of the action? A place where they feel inspired to do the best job they can possibly do and treat everyone around them in a way that makes them proud?

It can be summed up in one simple word: *respect.* People want to be respected by those who supervise them, work with them, are supervised by them and purchase from them.

It is not complicated. The concepts surrounding respect are actually very simple, and we all know them. Treat others with kindness, compassion, integrity and honesty. Do not ignore, dismiss or demean. Do not pre-judge . . . the list goes on and on.

But, here's the rub: because we all know these concepts, we take them for granted. We assume we are behaving respectfully toward others at all times – or at least most of the time – because that's "who we are" and who we want to be. Most of us achieve this goal most of the time.

The problem is that when we are stressed, overloaded, tired or ill, patience and respect are often the first things to go. When this happens, we often do not recognize our own disrespectful behavior toward others, partly because we can't control it while it is happening, but also because it contradicts what we consider to be our true, respectful nature. In other words, we often do not recognize it in ourselves, and when we do, we justify it after the fact "just this one time" because it only happens rarely, or because we were wronged first, or maybe just because we were having a bad day.

I would like to note here that there is a difference between behaving disrespectfully toward others *once in a while* (because we are so frustrated that it throws us "over the edge" and we just snap) and behaving disrespectfully as a matter of course. All of us behave in ways we don't really intend some of the time, no matter how hard we try not to go there. After all, we are not perfect, and we should not put added stress on ourselves to *be* perfect. But we need to periodically do a little introspection and look at our behavior patterns to determine whether we are behaving as respectfully as we *think* we are, as often as we want to do so, or if another behavior pattern has crept up on us without our noticing it. Sometimes we get ourselves into a pattern of disrespect because we are so stressed for so long that *disrespect* actually becomes our normal pattern of behavior. This could cause us to become exactly what we swore we would never be – bitter, disenchanted, cynical, and oppositional, and *that* causes us to be disrespectful toward others more often than not.

I saw an excellent YouTube video on customer service posted by Thomson Holidays in which a woman is dreaming of a vacation for herself and her son. She visits a travel agency to see what she can afford. Because the travel agent is apparently bored with her job, she practically dismisses everything the woman wants to do, and acts as though the customer is bothering her by asking her to find a vacation for herself and her son. The customer finally leaves the building with her dreams of a nice vacation obliterated. Later that night, the travel agent goes out to a restaurant with a friend. She and her friend are completely dismissed by the waiter, who acts as though they are bothering him to find them a clean table, take their order and treat them with respect. Suddenly, she recognizes how she disrespected her own customer that very afternoon with the same type of behavior. Finally realizing the devastating impact of her behavior on her customer, and resolved to fix the situation, she returns to work the next day, contacts the customer and helps her and her son get excited about their dream vacation. Her attitude was the only thing that changed, but it transformed everything because it allowed her to treat her customer with compassion and respect!

[If you want to see the video, search YouTube for *"Thomson Holiday Customer Service."*]

Effective Leaders Do Not Demand *Respect; They* Command *It*

As organizational leaders (this applies to leaders with and without titles), when we try to demand respect, it implies that we have not yet done anything to earn it. Respect is not automatically given to others (leaders or otherwise), nor should it be assumed or expected solely because of our title or "status." In fact, the very act of demanding respect actually lowers the respect others are willing to give us, usually causing them *not* to respect us.

Think about it: when was the last time you willingly did something demanded of you, especially by someone you did not respect? How did you feel about having to do it? Conversely, recall a time when something was requested of you by someone who had earned your respect. It is a very different motivation.

Therefore, we cannot *demand* respect; we must *command* it. The only thing we can and should reasonably demand is the benefit of the doubt; we should be able to expect others to give us a chance to prove that we are deserving of their respect. True respect is subsequently earned through our actions that prove we were *worthy* of receiving the benefit of the doubt.

Case in Point:

My husband and I once hosted a Japanese exchange student named Tomomi, whose family invited us to visit them during a vacation to Japan. Several weeks earlier, in Boston, we had met the high priest of the second-oldest temple in Japan. When he learned of our upcoming trip, he invited us to visit him there.

Upon arriving at Tomomi's home, we asked her to call this man to arrange for a meeting date and time, since I was not fluent enough in the Japanese language to confidently converse on the telephone. Tomomi did so, but was so fearful of using the wrong words to someone in his station in life that she "practiced" her conversation several times before placing the call! (In Japanese culture, each level of social position requires the use of special terms of respect when speaking to someone in a higher position. The appropriate terms are determined by the level of the person being addressed and the size of the "gap" between your positions.)

Upon visiting the high priest at his temple, we were in for a wonderful experience. But the biggest surprise came in the form of the extreme humility that he demonstrated, despite his high standing in Japanese society. I started out respecting him due to his station in life. However, my level of respect for him rose immeasurably when I saw how he treated everyone around him, regardless of their position. He was the high priest of the second-oldest temple in Japan. Not many Japanese citizens rank higher than this man in his country. Yet he did not *demand* respect of anyone; he *commanded* it through his actions, demeanor and words.

Everything about him was first-class. Although it was not necessary or expected for him to treat those in lower stations with respect, he did it anyway, earning a higher level of respect from everyone around him than he could have received by simply demanding respect due to his position without offering it in return.

As you can see, ideally, respect should flow both ways. However, some leaders believe that showing respect to those in lower positions is somehow beneath them. But this is not true. In fact, when leaders show true respect for everyone around them, including those at lower organizational levels where respect is so often withheld, the bond between leaders and followers is actually strengthened. Whether you are leading a company toward higher success, volunteering on a committee where you need to motivate all members to achieve a common goal; teaching a new generation how to be successful and responsible; or leading your family to be more productive, compassionate and caring members of society; bear in mind that effective leaders do not demand respect – they command it.

One final note on respect is that another way to show sensitivity and a true sense of "team" is for leaders to avoid using the term "subordinate" when referring to those who report to them. Additionally, if we're all working together toward the same goals, it is more respectful to say that associates work *with*, rather than *for*, a leader.

Go First

Sometimes other people are so difficult and nasty that they make it extremely difficult for us to treat them with respect. And there is often not much we can do about it. However, while we are not responsible for – nor can we control – how other people behave, we *can* control how we *react* to them, which is more than half the battle when it comes to respect. When we treat the other person with respect first, it sometimes changes their behavior for the better as well.

This scenario actually tests our skills and abilities the most. It is easy for us to behave respectfully when things go right. But how often can we count on that nowadays? Because so many things have the capacity to go wrong, a chain reaction of frustration, anger, and

77

resentment explodes outward in a staggering retaliatory show of disrespect to whomever happens to be unfortunate enough to serve as a handy target at the moment we "crack."

So, a customer calls about a problem with the company's product and verbally explodes on the representative who answers the phone.

Or a customer service representative explodes on the customer who has the misfortune of calling with a legitimate problem immediately following the call from the idiot who called to try to get extra products or services they neither paid for nor deserved.

Or a boss in a foul mood due to an argument with their spouse that morning negates the good mood of an associate who *started out* having a pretty good day.

Case in Point:

With a splitting headache, I pulled into a car rental lot, hauled my luggage out of the trunk, dragged it into the building, waited in line and went to the counter, when . . . ACCHH!!! I forgot to fill the gas tank! It was only three-quarters full. At that point, I had the painful choice of paying almost $9.00 per gallon plus a fuel service charge for them to fill it, or lugging my belongings back to the car, finding a gas station, filling the tank and driving back.

Ever cost-conscious, I chose the second option. When the attendant saw me come back to the car, I told her what happened, and she exclaimed, *"Oh no! I almost said something to remind you that the tank wasn't full, but I've had too many people yell and curse at me lately for doing exactly that, so I said to myself, 'Forget it! It's her problem!' and just ignored it. I'm really sorry."*

WOW, what an eye-opener! She thought about doing the right thing, and actually wanted to do it, but hesitated because too many customers had recently berated her for trying to go "above and beyond" to help them. She told me they've accused her of "trying to get into their business" and have even gotten angry with her because they knew their tank wasn't full, but were late for their flight and didn't need her "trying to make them feel stupid!" Really?

Customers so often blame customer service representatives for poor service, but the fact is that as the buying public becomes more and more rude to representatives who are simply trying to help, the representatives themselves are becoming more gun-shy about opening their mouths.

As customers become more rude, representatives become more gun-shy.

The big lesson here is that the more we hang on to the negative baggage that some people throw our way, the more we are tempted to assume that everyone is going to treat us that way, and we fail to give *anyone* the benefit of the doubt. Therefore, my challenge and plea to customer service representatives is to *go first*, and attempt to do the right thing anyway. Try to let rude customer actions roll off your back. Remember that each customer is different and should be treated as though they are coming to you with a "clean slate," really need your help, and will show gratitude rather than rudeness when it is offered.

My challenge and plea to customers is to try to *go first* and let the rude actions of previous customer service representatives roll off your back. Give these representatives the benefit of the doubt, treat them with dignity and remember that each one is different and should be treated as though they are coming to you with a "clean slate," have helpful intentions and will gladly offer the service you need.

And if that positive result does not happen, at least you won't be contributing to the cycle of rude behavior that threatens to cause negative customer service interactions to gather momentum and foster even *more* rude behavior in the future.

This is especially true when we are dealing with those who have been beaten down the most in life, or do not have the experience or maturity to make the difficult decision to go first.

Case in Point:

There are two excellent movies that also show us the value of both going first and commanding respect, rather than demanding it. They are *"The Freedom Writers"* and *"The Ron Clark Story."* They both relate the story of teachers who went into inner-city schools to try to reduce drop-out rates and help the students gain the necessary education to become productive citizens.

However, because of the horrendous life experiences these students had already experienced, they did not trust any adults, especially teachers in their schools. Thus, when the new teacher arrived, their goal was to disrespect enough to force that teacher to quit and let the students "mess up" their lives as they wished. As a result, if these teachers were going to be effective, they were going to have to back off and find another way to reach their students.

They did it by showing respect to the students first, and gaining their respect in return. They did not view this action as backing down in any way. Although in the eyes of their students they appeared to be doing so and "losing," they actually succeeded in gaining the respect, trust and admiration of those students, allowing them to achieve their long-term goals of teaching and guiding the students to success.

We can take a lesson from these teachers, who expressed care and compassion, and *earned* the respect of their students by showing them respect before actually receiving the respect they themselves deserved. If we decide to *go first* and stop demanding respect from others before being willing to give it – if we become more willing to make the first move and give respect, or at least the benefit of the doubt – we will not only help turn our workplaces into **WOWplaces**, but we may begin taking steps to help our society move forward and grow, as well.

*One Final **WOW** of Going First: A **WOWplace** does not just give* back; *it gives* before!

Our world is currently more focused on charitable giving than at any time in history. Everywhere you go, you see and hear the challenge to give back. Well, I say, *"Don't wait until you've gotten first so you can give back. Give before!"* Not just in terms of money, but in terms of time, energy, caring, compassion and a commitment to doing the right thing at the right time. Even if you can't afford to give money at any given time, you can always give of your time and talents, which are often more valuable and needed than money.

Give before, not just because you want to *get* more, but in the true spirit of giving without expectation of reward. What I have found is that when I have given first, without expecting something back, I have always gotten more because it is very true that "what goes around comes around."

Internal Customers Require Respect, Too

Whenever we think of customer service, we automatically think of external customers who buy our products and services. However, in order to accomplish our goal of gaining their loyalty and winning even more customers, we must also realize and remember that *internal* customers require and deserve the same level of service and respect we ask them to give *external* customers.

Internal customers are defined as co-workers who need something from us, whether it be information, products, reports, policies or other goods and services, in order to do their job to the best of their ability. For example, if I work in Marketing and need information from the Manufacturing department regarding when new products will be ready, I am an internal customer of Manufacturing. Anyone who uses a computer program is an internal customer of Information Technology. And since none of us want to work for free, all associates are internal customers of the Payroll Department!

Only when all associates treat each other with respect, by providing co-workers with required items and information in a timely and cordial manner, can everyone help the organization achieve its goal of treating external customers with the service and respect they deserve. This applies to every associate, at every level. No one, no matter how high level a position they hold, is exempt from the need to show respect to others.

Backing Off Does Not Equal Backing Down: Our Absurdly High Fear of "Losing Face"

IBM vs. Mac? Cat person or dog person? Democrat, Republican or Independent?

How many times do we fail to "back off" on an opinion, comment, or even our own food, computer or pet preferences, simply because we equate "backing off" with "backing down?" How many situations escalate and cause harm to all parties involved because everyone is trying to win and avoid "losing face?" Have you ever been in a situation where you have experienced sleepless nights, excessive worry, agitation, and fear due to someone's (or your own) need to win at all costs?

Too many people are so concerned about backing down that they absolutely refuse to back off . . . ever! They keep pushing and pushing (and pushing!) until the situation becomes toxic, or even explosive, in their efforts to get everyone to agree with them, rather than "bowing" to another's will by letting anyone have a differing opinion.

Too many people are so concerned about backing down that they absolutely refuse to back off . . . ever!

Allowing another person to have their own opinion, i.e., showing them respect by realizing they are entitled to that opinion, is not the same as backing down and changing our own. Actually, we should all practice being open-minded enough to consider viewpoints that differ from ours and see if they might offer enlightenment. They may cause us to change our minds, or they may actually strengthen our own position. But the worst thing we can do is to close our minds and refuse to show at least common courtesy (which, by the way, is becoming less and less common) to those who hold differing opinions.

This situation is difficult enough in our personal lives, but when we allow disrespectful interactions to occur at work, it damages our work relationships, as well as our work products and work environment, which can lead to widespread reduction of the effectiveness of everyone there.

So, instead of arguing our opinions "to the death" at all costs, we can agree to:

- ◉ **Pick our battles.** Do not argue every point, simply because there is a difference of opinion. Does it really matter if they like Mac and we like IBM, or vice versa? Is it worth the aggravation all parties will feel by becoming involved in unnecessary arguments? If a matter is small or inconsequential, who cares? Healthy debate is a good thing, but taking it too far can lead to trouble. If you simply do not agree, let them have their opinion and just get along with each other. Allowing someone to have their own opinion does not mean you agree with it! It just means you respect their right to have it.

- ◉ **Remain respectful.** When the matter is important enough, remember that regardless of how "wrong" (☺) they are, they have as much right to their opinion as we do to ours. We must remain respectful as we listen to their position and explain

83

ours. If we show respect during a disagreement, the other party will be more willing to listen and reciprocate with respect, enabling a possible learning experience, rather than just a debilitating exercise in frustration!

◉ **Agree to disagree.** If it becomes apparent that we will not see eye-to-eye on the issue, find a way to "agree to disagree," or seek a compromise that poses a solution where we can both win and then move on.

Think about how this relates to your real life situations. How many real estate transactions have blown up because neither buyer nor seller would back off due to a fear of appearing weak and backing down, causing both parties to lose sight of their goals and lose the sale in an effort to avoid losing face? How many families have family members who stop talking to each other because their only way of communicating is to belittle and demean others in an effort to dominate and "win?" How many workplaces are run by intimidation and fear, rather than collaboration and respect?

There are many ways to accomplish almost anything. We are not put on this earth to "put other people in their place" or slam them down so hard that they stay there simply because their opinion differs from ours. Our goal in life should not be to belittle, embarrass or berate others. It should be to lift others up, encourage them, and make them feel valued, as we create a better world together.

Our world – and our workplaces – will become much bigger **WOWplaces** if we keep in mind how we feel when others berate us, and stop equating backing off out of respect for others' opinions, with backing down and losing face with regard to our own.

Respect is Everything!

Quite simply, respect is everything. Without it, you do not engage associates, you do not retain customers, and you do not build a team that remains cohesive and mutually strives for higher results. Respect is the glue that holds an organization together and creates an atmosphere and a culture where people want to work. But respect must be continuously earned and maintained.

Of course an organization can be built without respect. But constant turnover and its associated expenses and stresses will be a continuing issue as associates move in and out of the organization. And it will never keep a team of people together long enough to become familiar enough with its products, services and culture to spot the gaps where anyone could do better.

Commanding respect from associates means, among other things:

◉ Paying them a competitive wage.

◉ Knowing what associates want well enough to offer them a variety of benefits that they will value.

◉ Listening to their ideas, applying them if appropriate, then giving them credit where credit is due.

◉ Rewarding them for thinking proactively and compassionately to make everything better for co-workers, as well as customers.

Commanding respect from customers means, among other things:

◉ Listening to their complaints without pre-judging them as "complainers" or "idiots."

◉ Acting on their legitimate complaints in a timely manner . . . or at all.

◉ Submitting their good suggestions, even if you are not sure they can be accomplished, then going one step further and finding a way to let them know you have considered the suggestion and acted on it, if appropriate.

◉ Returning their calls when promised.

◉ Ensuring that every sales and service representative knows your products and services extremely well, so they don't promise what you can't deliver.

Nine Tips for Commanding Respect

1. **Respect other people's time.** For example, when making requests of others, ask for necessary details, but do not overwhelm them with unnecessary requests, simply for the sake of having them provide more details than needed. Explain why requests are made, and involve them (if possible) in deciding what is needed and what is not. If you must provide them with information, give them what they need, in the format in which they need it. Do not waste their time by overwhelming them with unnecessary details.

2. **Respect their wishes.** You may not always agree with their wishes, but (barring anything illegal) you must respect their right to have and act upon them.

3. **Respect their communication style.** Everyone communicates differently, and many differences exist among people of varying backgrounds. For example, when people of Mediterranean heritage are excited, they may raise their voice in excitement or passion, which may be mistaken for anger by someone of a more restrained background who shows little outward emotion, even when excited. *Never* assume that a negative reaction is taking place just because someone reacts differently than you would to any given situation. I have experienced occasions

where someone thought I was getting upset about something (due to my Italian background) when I was just getting excited!

4. **Respect their knowledge and experience.** Allow them to participate as early as possible in any process, and lend their experience to help the project succeed. If someone has more experience and success than you do, sit quietly and listen to them, regardless of their age.

5. **Respect their right to their own opinions,** even if you do not agree with them. No one wants "yes-men" all around them (well, maybe sometimes we do, but we shouldn't). If we surround ourselves with people who never disagree with our opinions, how will we ever grow?

6. **Respect their efforts to learn, grow and change**, and give them some time and space to do so. Encourage them to grow their knowledge and expertise. Don't stifle their dreams, even if you do not share their passion for that dream.

7. **Give the other person your full attention.** People do not feel respected when they know they are not really being listened to, or worse, being placated or patronized. Maintain appropriate eye contact, limit gestures that indicate nervousness or impatience (such as finger tapping or looking around at your surroundings) and let them know you value their time and offerings.

8. **When you ask for help, come full circle.** This is especially important in situations such as the aforementioned suggestion box, which many associates feel are "black holes" where suggestions go in, but nothing comes out. Whether you implement associate suggestions or not, take the time to communicate back to them whether or not their suggestion will be implemented, and the reasons why (or why not). Let them know you are listening by letting them know their ideas and suggestions are

not falling on deaf ears. Customers who offer suggestions often feel the same way. I am sure most companies never *intend* to ignore associate or customer comments. I would even wager that many companies would even be tempted to believe, *"That would never happen here!"* But when managers raise issues and ask for suggestions and ideas without following through, unfortunate incidents can occur due to inadvertent messages, bad assumptions and lack of communication.

9. **Give credit when and where it is due.** Another common statement that reflects a feeling of disrespect is, *"My supervisor takes credit for whatever I do anyway, so I don't offer my ideas any more."* Rather than running with someone else's idea and failing to acknowledge their input, leaders must be secure enough in their own position and abilities to allow others to contribute and receive credit for doing so. In fact, it is a high compliment to the leader when others are willing to work hard, be creative and lend a helping hand to make that leader – and their department or company – look good. By leading associates to higher levels of productivity and creativity, we can take credit for being great leaders, rather than having to take credit simply for one good idea.

Leaders should take credit for being great leaders, rather than simply for one good idea

Some Quick Notes on Giving People Your Full Attention

Picture this: You go to a social or networking event and meet someone you know. You walk up to her and stretch out your hand to shake theirs and say hello. They give you a quick cursory glance, but as you start to speak, their eyes begin darting around the room, looking for other people to approach, so they don't miss saying hello to anyone else. Now, don't you feel really *special*?

Or, just as you have been informed of a problem in one area of the workplace that requires your attention, one of your co-workers comes to you with a different question or problem. The associate insists that they need to talk to you now, and you do not want that person to feel as though you're not interested in what they have to say. You assume it will just take a minute, but as the minutes drag on, and you realize the conversation will take much longer than expected, you become agitated, impatient and anxious for it to be finished, and the matter settled. In your earnestness to "handle" the problem quickly, you end up making your co-worker feel "handled," but not particularly valued or listened to. They felt placated, resentful and regretful for bringing the issue to you. This promotes a pervasive sense infecting many workplaces: *"They never listen to me and don't care anyway, so why bother?"* Even worse, the sentiment that "no good deed goes un-punished" is reinforced.

All your good intentions of valuing workers by trying to quickly resolve their issues and making them feel important are for naught, as you inadvertently accomplish the exact opposite of what was intended. Instead of trying to handle things "on the fly," ask up front if the issue is so urgent that it cannot wait until the first emergency is handled. If so, you will have a decision to make: tackle this issue and get word to the first set of associates that you will be in to handle their issue shortly, or delegate one of the issues. If not, inform them of the immediate problem you are currently on your way to handle. Tell them that although you cannot currently give them your full attention, you want to set up a time to meet once you have returned.

By setting expectations up front – for yourself and your associate – and communicating the reason for your inability to speak with them in depth at that moment, you avoid inadvertent messages of disrespect to either party, allowing each to reasonably anticipate and respect what you are doing and why. This lessens the stress of trying to do too many things at one time . . . none of them well.

Chapter Summary:
How to WOW Through Making the WOWplace Respectful

1. Effective leaders do not demand respect; they command it.

2. Go First.

3. One Final **WOW** of Going First: A **WOWplace** does not just give back; it gives before!

4. Internal customers require respect, too.

5. Backing off does not equal backing down: our absurdly high fear of "losing face."

6. Respect is everything!

7. Nine tips for commanding respect.

   a. Respect other people's time.

   b. Respect their wishes.

   c. Respect their communication style.

   d. Respect their knowledge and experience.

   e. Respect their right to their own opinion.

   f. Respect their efforts to learn, grow and change.

   g. Give the other person your full attention.

   h. When you ask for help, come full circle.

   i. Give credit when and where it is due.

8. Some quick notes on giving people your full attention.

We do not want to turn off our humanity when we step through the doors of the workplace.

Chapter Five:

WOWplace Rule #3

A **WOWplace** is Human . . .

Not Humanoid

A **WOWplace** is Human . . . Not Humanoid

There is an old saying that people don't leave *companies,* they leave *people.* Think about it: what is a company but a group of people who gather to create an entity that reflects who they are and what they value?

Associates don't work for a "company." They may be attracted by what the company has to offer, and want to help the company prosper and grow, but the fact is that they work for and with *people.* And just as employers are disappointed when they hire an associate who "interviewed well" but does not live up to the standards they professed in the interview, the same is true for associates who interview with Dr. Jekyll, only to find that they have signed on with Mr. Hyde when they report to work every day. It goes both ways.

One high-level executive who does not follow the **WOWplace** Rules can poison an entire workplace. One manager or supervisor who behaves in a way that is inconsistent with what they say can demotivate an entire division or department. And one associate who comes to work in a foul mood, or with an attitude of entitlement rather than achievement, can make an entire team become unproductive and disillusioned. And like the ebb and flow of the tides in the ocean, it spreads to every customer who interacts with them.

Be Human . . . Not Humanoid

Many of us know of Mr. Spock, a central character on *Star Trek,* the popular television show created in the 1960s and still popular today. As were many of the characters in this futuristic show, Mr. Spock was partly extra-terrestrial. He was half human and half Vulcan. Vulcans have trained themselves to eliminate all emotion, so even though he looked human, Mr. Spock was very unemotional in his dealings. Occasionally, his "human side" tried to emerge, but Spock strove valiantly to overcome this tendency, since Vulcans considered any emotion to be a character flaw.

If you are a real "Trekker" you also know of another character named Data, who starred in the sequel series, *Star Trek: The Next Generation.* Data was really an android that looked human, but because he was an android, also did not feel human emotions.

Both of these humanoids were *extremely* competent at their jobs, and both were completely incapable of feeling or displaying human emotion. While it might be tempting to dream of working with them on a starship at some point in time light years in the future, the fact is that all of us earthlings are, at heart and at our core, human; complete with feelings and emotions that seek to be satisfied. We want to laugh, we want to joke, we want to feel and share our emotions with other human beings! We do *not* want to turn off our humanity when we step through the doors to the workplace . . . nor should we.

Being human, and strengthening the connection of a team of people, makes going to work worthwhile.

Being human and strengthening the human connection of a team of people passionately committed to creating **WOW** experiences for everyone around us is what makes getting up and going to work worthwhile.

I am sure we've all worked with – and for – humanoids at one point or another. We encounter them everywhere: in our offices; on the roads; even in the grocery store, working as cashiers or baggers in the checkout lane. You make a joke, but they don't laugh! They just stare at you, ignore you, or look at you as if you have two heads simply because you want to have a little fun while you're there. They are not interested in either having fun themselves or allowing you to do so.

By contrast, when you visit a place where *humans* work in the checkout lanes, humans who smile and speak to you, interact with you, maybe even laugh and share a small joke or other form of human emotion with you, it completely transforms your experience into one you want to repeat and share with others.

Job Duties vs. Human Duties

Upon encountering a humanoid in the workplace, you hope for some human compassion, kindness or understanding, but they have none to give. You may even hear them justify their behavior by saying, *"Hey, I'm just here to do my job. It's not my job to make people feel good! I'm not their Mom or Dad!"* You may also hear, *"No one worries about how I feel, so why should I worry about them?"*

That is workplace thinking! **WOWplace** thinking reinforces the concept that while it is not necessarily our job to make people feel *good*, it is also not our job to make them feel

While we have job duties to perform, we also have human duties that accompany every aspect of our job.

97

bad, which can inadvertently happen when we focus solely on one half of the equation, but not the other, which is: while we have *job duties* to perform at work, we also have *human duties* that accompany every aspect of our job.

Case in Point:

I once visited a company where I was early for a meeting. As I waited in the lobby, the receptionist left her desk to run an errand. While she was gone, a man arrived and stood at the desk, waiting for someone to help him. Before the receptionist returned, another associate emerged from a back room and went behind the desk. The visitor, thinking this was the receptionist, straightened up and prepared to talk to her when she looked up to take care of him.

She never did! She looked in a Rolodex, rifled through some papers, and opened a file drawer. As time passed, the man's posture drooped, for he realized that not only was this woman *not* going to help him, she was not even going to *acknowledge* him! After about two minutes, she left the reception area, not once acknowledging anyone in the lobby or the man standing right in front of her!

When the receptionist returned she took care of the man, but what had happened by then? A company visitor had been forced to stand and wait while a company associate disrespected both his presence and his needs, not even showing him the *common courtesy* of acknowledging him. He also experienced consternation as he worried about "interrupting" an associate who should have been worried about *him.*

I don't know what was going through that associate's mind at that moment. Maybe she was too intent on what she was doing to notice her surroundings. More likely, she figured that since it was not her job to handle the reception area, she didn't need to bother acknowledging the visitor.

Either way, how difficult would it have been for her to acknow-ledge and help him? In one or two sentences, she could have shown him courtesy and respect and helped him; at the very least, simply by *not* ignoring him, she could have bought the receptionist more time to return and help him.

We sometimes forget that our jobs are not performed in a vacuum. Humans exist all around us, whether or not our immediate task directly involves them. Therefore, even if we do not have a *job* duty to the person in front of us, we have a *human* duty to respect and show common courtesy to *everyone* in front of us. If we want to create **WOW** experiences, we must remember that our job duties are performed *by* humans, *with* humans and *for* humans. How we interact with them makes all the difference in determining whether or not their experience is a positive one.

For example, in the previous *Case in Point,* the worker who ignored the visitor at the reception desk may be very good at performing her own job. She may even be the kind of associate everyone wants to hire: someone who never says, *"It's not my job!"* when asked to help in another area, who offers to help when she recognizes an obvious opportunity to pitch in and get a job done. She may also have been horrified if she had ever witnessed someone else do what she had done to that visitor, or if it had happened to her as a visitor in another establishment. But she didn't recognize it in herself.

The less obvious situations that "fly under the radar" are the ones we often miss. They usually happen when we are distracted, busy, upset over something else, or in an unfamiliar position. We frequently get "tunnel vision" as we focus on trying to complete a particular task. Our failure to recognize opportunities to be human and create a **WOW** often results in an OW instead.

Do visitors at a reception desk care who says "Hello" to them? Of course not! But they do care deeply if *no one* says it, or does anything to acknowledge them at all. They simply want someone to acknowledge that there is a human being in the room! We all want to be treated with respect, rather than as though we are invisible, unimportant or "just one more annoyance standing there, asking for something!"

Here is how these Job Duties and Human Duties differ:

Job Duties focus on tasks and skills: how well we know our job functions; how competently we perform the technical and functional aspects of the job; how well we know and follow company policy; and how knowledgeable and expert we have become at performing our jobs. We have all heard of the "Can Do" attitude. Job Duties focus on what we *can* do and *how well* we do it.

Job duties focus on what we can do and how well we do it.

Human duties focus on what we will do and how we do it.

Human Duties focus on attitudes and values: what our values are, how we treat other people and *how* we do our jobs. For example, human duties focus on how well leaders keep humans in mind when *creating* company policy, rather than on how well associates know and follow that policy. In addition, they focus on how we interact and communicate with co-workers at every level of the organization as we perform the tasks at hand. Whereas job duties simply focus on what we *can* do and how well we do it, human duties are really about what we *will* do in any given situation. Therefore, human duties focus on what we *will* do and *how* we do it.

Human Leaders Create *WOWs*

Focusing on our human duties entails what we are willing to do to emotionally connect with others, even if those things are not required of the job. They are actions that go over and above, but demonstrate who and what we really are.

Case in Point:

I once worked for the president of a U.S. Division with 2,000 associates. He worked in two main offices – one on the East Coast and one on the West Coast – so every two weeks he flew back and forth to perform his duties in each location. Needless to say, he was extremely busy.

However, each December he took the time to pen a handwritten note inside greeting cards to all 2,000 associates. The note was not just a generic *"Happy Holidays!"* message. If he knew an associate personally – which he usually made a point of doing – some personal aspect of whatever he knew about that individual or his family was referenced in the note. If he didn't know them, he wrote a "welcoming" note or other appropriate message to show he cared about writing something meaningful to them.

In order to get all the cards done in time for the holidays, he began writing these notes two months in advance. He took them on every plane ride and wrote notes all the way across the country, as well as whenever he had time around the rest of his workload. He took the cards home and wrote notes in his limited free time there. He even carried them with him for every meeting outside the office, just in case he had a few minutes to write one or two while he waited for the meeting to start.

All associates marveled at this wonderful act of caring and humanity because they knew how busy the president was. The fact that he took the time to do it every year was one more action that endeared him to his people, who responded by giving him their very best work.

A Little Humility Goes a Long Way

Another factor that endears this president to his people is his humility. He never talks down to his staff, does not act as though tasks or projects are beneath him, and is always accessible to everyone in the organization. When you compare the actions and attitudes of this type of leader with those who demand special treatment at every step – even to the inconvenience or detriment of others – you see how much more respect leaders who maintain their humility command, than those who seem to believe everyone owes them special treatment.

Some of the greatest leaders in the world have gone on to greatness while still remaining grounded and humble. One who comes to mind is David Packard, co-founder of Hewlett-Packard, who practiced the art of "management by walking around." His practice of acknowledging and respecting his associates' dignity as human beings resulted in a dedicated culture of associates who helped create a competitive advantage, and deliver 40 consecutive years of profitable growth.

This does not mean that humble leaders are meek or lacking in confidence. But it *does* mean that they understand they are not the only ones with good ideas that should at least be heard, even if not developed. It also means that if they are wrong, they can not only recognize but admit it in order to correct a situation and move on. Admitting a mistake is sometimes viewed as a weakness, but in reality, when leaders possess enough humility and honesty to admit and correct a mistake, it adds legitimacy and credibility to their leadership, and allows others to view them in a more realistic and human light. This binds them more strongly to that leader because no one is perfect. Admitting this fact breaks down at least one very large barrier to complete trust in the leader.

In fact, why is it that some people can get others to *want* to work for them so badly that they don't care what position they have to take to do so, while others can't get anyone to want to work for them, no matter how good the position is? It is because exceptional leaders are *human* and they possess qualities that make them humble, compassionate and enjoyable to work with and be around!

Case in Point:

An executive at a large hospital was soon to head up a new hospital within his current system. Associates who worked for the organization began lining up to go with him when he opened the doors. He heard comments like, *"You're taking me with you when you go, right?"* and *"I don't care what the position is, when you open that hospital, I want to work for you!"*

Unfortunately, he had more associates asking to go with him than he had positions to fill. **WOW,** what a problem to have! But it is what his associates told us about what this leader does that makes everyone want to work for him:

"He respects us and asks for our input, and then he actually uses it!"

"He's a lot of fun to work for, not stuffy and stodgy, and has a great sense of humor!"

"He always takes time to show everyone that he really cares about us as people."

"He really knows his stuff, but he doesn't act like he's better than everyone else."

These comments exemplify the statistic that reveals that the second main reason associates are attracted to a particular workplace (or in this case to a particular leader) is "working for competent management teams with leaders who are considerate." They highlight the traits that effective leaders display on a consistent basis. Note that these associates do not want to work for a different organization; they want to work for the same organization, and specifically for him. *He* is the main factor in creating the **WOWplace**!

This leader actually exemplifies the inverse of the saying, *"People don't leave companies; they leave people,"* which is that *"People don't want to work just for a good company; they want to work for good people."* We can work for the best company in the world, but if the people we work directly with are not good people, it does not matter how good the company is. It's just not worth it.

The Seemingly Paradoxical Benefit of Being Human in a Leadership Position

Sometimes people equate being professional and "leader-like" with being impassive and unemotional. But there is room for both leadership and emotion in the **WOWplace**. Leaders do need to keep their emotions in check, but they must be careful not to become unapproachable to those they work with or lead. This means that they must be human enough for associates to be willing to "go to the wall" for them when necessary or appropriate, which they won't do for an unemotional "humanoid" they only know at arm's length. They will do it for someone they care about, and who they are absolutely confident cares about them.

Returning once more to the *Star Trek* theme, one very interesting piece of trivia demonstrates the power of our innate humanity and how much impact it generates when leaders occasionally allow it to show. Even though leaders must maintain strict control over their emotions in the workplace in order to effectively lead their people, much like a Starship Captain must do on board the ship, it is important to note that even *they* are human, and most effective as leaders when they *show it* from time to time.

This was clearly demonstrated in a 2006 Christie's auction of *Star Trek* memorabilia. Among the items up for auction was a Ressikan flute played by Captain Jean Luc Picard of *Star Trek: The Next Generation* in an episode in which he entered the life of another man who lived a simple existence in a village on another planet.

The "flute" was actually an inoperable wooden prop that should have been "forgotten" as inconsequential, as it represented only one *tiny* piece of memorabilia among thousands of pieces from five TV seasons and several full-length movies. And yet, it received a bid for $40,000! Why? Because fans had connected so strongly with Jean Luc's more sensitive side – his *human* side – that it impacted them deeply when he played the flute during that episode. It stayed in their minds, and more importantly their hearts, for over 20 years. Its significance remained unknown all that time, until it went up for auction and its emotional impact was revealed.

When leaders are strong, confident and in control, but also human, their humanity brings people together, binds them to the organization and to each other, and inspires them to become a team working to reach a common goal. When they behave as though there is no place for humanity or emotion in the workplace, they disengage themselves from the very humans they wish to lead.

And until we actually discover and begin to work with beings from other planets who interact differently than humans do, the only way to turn our workplace into a **WOWplace** is to *be* human, rather than simply *imitating* humans. We must take care not to get so caught up in our job duties and tasks that we forget about the human duties that exist whether we are on the job, off the job (or even in our own homes) that always exist and are always appreciated.

The Promotion Phenomenon

One example of the power of focusing on both job duties and human duties is reflected in this question: Why do so many great associates get promoted to supervisory and management positions because they excelled *technically* in their previous jobs, only to fail miserably as leaders once there?

The answer lies in the fact that too much emphasis is usually placed on their job duties (the technical aspects of performing their current job), with too little focus on the human duties that would have prepared them for success beyond that position.

Without the leadership skills necessary for the new position, they often fall back on what they know and feel comfortable doing, namely the job duties they previously mastered, with the following results:

- **Failure to appropriately delegate.** They do not know how to delegate; they are used to doing things, not assigning things for others to do.

- **Missed deadlines.** They fall back into their comfort zone of actually performing tasks, rather than leading and motivating the people now responsible for performing them.

- **Micromanagement.** Since they do not know how to properly delegate and let team members do their jobs, they constantly monitor the team, often dictating how to do every minute aspect of each task, rather than giving them a goal and guidelines to follow, and only dictating absolutes when necessary.

- **Loss of confidence from the team.** Since the leader seems to have no confidence in their abilities to do their jobs, they worry about whether they'll be successful, or if the team's failure will reflect badly on them personally. This can cause anxiety, fear, the stifling of creativity and positive risk, and other negative team attitudes and behaviors.

- **Frustration and loss of self-confidence.** They fear an inability to perform the new job adequately or comfortably.

If there is no management focus on instilling and developing human duties (more specifically defined as expanded versions of "soft skills") across all levels of the organization, most associates neither learn these skills for themselves, nor see them demonstrated in their current leaders. A workplace will never become a **WOWplace** if we continue the cycle of taking people out of jobs at which they technically excel, and promoting them to jobs for which they are not emotionally prepared.

Associates may come across a few "natural" leaders who demonstrate these traits. We all know who they are because *everyone* wants to work with them. But we cannot expect a few natural leaders to compensate for those who have never been taught how to be effective *human* leaders.

Arrogance vs. Confidence

An important nuance of humanity and leadership that should also be discussed is the distinction between arrogance and confidence in the workplace and in our dealings with others. While arrogance can play an important role in certain situations, it has absolutely no place in others. For example, many consider it incredibly arrogant for doctors to believe they can accomplish some of the miracles that have been done, such as brain surgery, open heart surgery and organ transplants. Before it was proven to be possible, some even considered it not only extremely arrogant but absolute "blasphemy" for doctors to even consider stopping a heart, repairing or replacing it and then bringing a person back to life. But the arrogance (a.k.a., confidence that is unfathomable for most of us) of these doctors has made it possible to sustain and prolong life in circumstances previously believed terminal.

However, while arrogance plays a significant role in the accomplishment of the surgery and other life-giving procedures, it has absolutely no place in the bedside manner of any physician when trying to explain a procedure and its benefits and risks, or comfort patients and their loved ones before or after that procedure. No matter how skilled a surgeon may be, there is no place – and no call – for a complete lack of humility and humanity when dealing with other human beings. It is my hope that the sentiment embodied in the statement, *"He may have a horrible bedside manner, but he is a very good doctor"* will quickly make way for the sentiment, *"He is an excellent doctor and his bedside manner is exceptional, as well. Not only did he treat me well as a patient, but he also treated me as a human being in the process."*

The same holds true for business leaders. In an era where much competitive advantage lies in our ability to motivate others, being a more human, compassionate and humble leader attracts others to us and helps bring out the best in them, creating a win for everyone.

WOWers Act According to Their Values (a.k.a. Victor's Values)

Part of being human means we are compelled to act according to our values and answer the question, *"Will I Or Won't I?"* with *"I will!"*

Case in Point:

I was in Chicago for a speaking engagement when my back went out and I ended up on the floor in front of the hotel elevator. Obviously, I wasn't planning to go to a hospital, so I told them not to call 911. But given our current litigious atmosphere and their fear that I would bring a lawsuit against them, they called 911. After signing forms waiving medical help, I managed to get on my feet, do my program and get to the airport for the trip home. But by the time I got there, I was physically, mentally and emotionally exhausted, and about at the end of my rope, when I began the long trek to my gate at that *tiny* little airport known as O'Hare.

Suddenly, as I began to feel my back and legs go out again, two Good Samaritans rushed up to keep me from falling. As we tried to decide what to do, the driver of a nearby airline travel cart noticed us and came over to inquire if we needed help. He asked my name, and when I told him, he said, *"Hi, Sandy. My name is Victor. I'm going to help you get home. Everything is going to be all right."* And for the first time since crumpling into a heap that morning, I actually began to believe it *would* be!

I looked up at the face of what must have been a guardian angel sent to help me and almost cried with relief, realizing that I wasn't on my own any more, when I just didn't have the strength to continue. But Victor helped me continue. He stayed with me for an hour and a half, since you never know when the gate for a flight will be changed – which mine was. He then arranged for a narrow airplane aisle chair to be brought to my gate in case I needed help getting to my seat on the plane. He even called ahead to Orlando to arrange for a wheelchair there, which I hadn't even thought of; but Victor thought ahead for me.

As Victor helped me every step of the way, making all the arrangements I needed *all the way through my journey to Orlando*, I thanked him and told him he must be my guardian angel, to which he replied, *"Well, that's the way my Momma raised me."*

That statement said it all. In one sentence, Victor showed me his true values – and demonstrated his commitment to showing those values to everyone he meets . . . even total strangers.

While you may say that Victor's *job* dictated that he helps everyone he meets (even total strangers), Victor's *values* dictated *how* he did that job. That's really the most important point, isn't it? *How* we do our jobs? *How* we live our lives? Do we really want to just do our jobs or live our lives, simply going through the motions to get from Point A to Point B? Or do we really care about the people we come in contact with every day, and let that care and compassion – our *values* (*Victor's* values) – shine through in everything we say and do?

Wouldn't we all have better places to live and work together if we helped create more "Victors" and fewer "Victims?" Too many of us fall victim to poor values and service from people who do not possess, or even if they *do* possess, fail to *exhibit* Victor's values in their lives.

It's not hard to create a **WOW** by acting according to our values. Even the most seemingly trivial of actions on our part can make a monumental difference to someone else in need of that particular action at that particular moment. It's up to us to create a true victory, by acting according to our *values,* and not necessarily according to our *mood*, each time we have a choice to either remain complacent and do nothing, or possibly create a **WOW** for someone else.

It's up to us to act according to our values, and not according to our mood.

Victor created an incredible **WOW** for me – not because he had to do it, or was paid to do it, but simply because he was someone who acted according to his *values*.

The Importance of Proactive Thinking in Creating the **WOW**

Victor's values and his concern for my well-being allowed him to think several steps beyond my immediate needs, to everything I would require from anyone at any time during that trip. In doing so, he demonstrated extraordinary proactive thinking skills on behalf of another person. He thought about what would happen if my gate changed, the problem I might have walking down the aisle to get to my seat on the plane, and even what would happen when I arrived back in Orlando. How would I be able to get off the plane, retrieve my luggage and get myself to whatever transportation I needed?

What if more of us followed Victor's example and took the time to think proactively for others, especially when they can't do it for themselves? What kind of experiences could we create if we began to think about *their* needs to such a degree that it left no doubt that we care about them and put their needs *first*, even long after our interaction with them is over? It is the small nuances and our capability and willingness to consider and perform them that truly separate those who are dedicated to creating **WOW** experiences from those who are not.

How do we combine the concepts of proactive thinking and compassion to create more Victors and fewer Victims? You can use the "Aim for the **WOW**!" target for this exercise. However, below is another formula to help guide your proactive thinking even further when you are trying to go over and above. I call it the 1-2-3s of Doing More Than Appease.

The 1-2-3s of Doing More Than Appease

We all know what "over and above" means conceptually. In general terms, it means going beyond what is expected, or beyond what the average person would do in any given situation.

But what does it mean *specifically?* How do we create it? Does it just occur by some fantastic collision of wonderful, but haphazard events? Or is it something we can plan on, prepare for and systematically create?

Keeping in mind that the **WOW** only happens – in fact, *can only happen* – when "over and above" is present in a specific situation, how do we ensure that it happens intentionally and consistently, rather than by happy accident or fortunate mistake?

What if there was a formula we could follow for creating the **WOW** on a consistent basis, that outlined specific actions we could take – as individuals and as an organization as a whole – in order to create the **WOW** and have it become *planned enough* to be effective, instantaneous and easily applied when needed and appropriate, without appearing to be prescriptive or "canned?"

I have created a deceptively straightforward, easy-to-remember and simple-to-execute three-step formula based on the concept of "over and above" that everyone can learn and apply in order to create the **WOW**. It is based on three simple questions we can all ask ourselves in any service situation.

Question #1: What Can I Do Now?

This is the question we all ask ourselves whenever a customer service situation arises. In fact, this is the point at which something is expected and usually performed because it is the routine and expected response to the customer service issues that arise every day. It is reactive and literally cannot be avoided, so most companies and associates worth their salt do have an answer for this question, even if just to appease the customer.

One problem is that although this is the easiest step, there are still too many companies and their associates who fall short and fail to ask even this most basic question. The bigger problem is that even when customer service representatives *do* ask and answer this first question, most consider their job done at this point. However, this step is the basic minimum, and should be considered only the *beginning* of the process, not the *end* of it!

Therefore, those who want to create a **WOW** must go on to the second question.

Question #2: What Else Can I Do Now?

This second question is proactive and addresses customer needs, not only at the initial point of customer service intervention, but even after that first level of service has been provided. It is the question most people do not even think to ask because they don't think it is necessary. But **WOW**s almost never happen when just the bare minimum of expectations are met. They only occur in the land of "over and above."

This step is where we begin to create the **WOW,** because it is where we start to take into account the nuances that create **WOW** experiences.

Question #3: What Else Can I Do *Later*, or *For* Later?

To finalize the **WOW,** we must proceed to Question #3: What else can I do *later*, or *for* later? This step requires much further proactive thinking on behalf of someone else, to create a continual or repeat **WOW** in the near or far future; not just at the beginning of the process, but all the way through the entire service transaction, which could span hours, days or even weeks.

It is the one superlative action that causes someone to be so positively impacted by their experience with you that they do not forget about it, and cannot help but talk about it to everyone they know.

Applying the 1-2-3 Formula to Victor's Values

In my previous story of Victor, the airline travel cart driver who helped me at O'Hare, we can see the 1-2-3s of Doing More Than Appease in action. Victor took care of my immediate need *(What can I do now?)* by getting me a wheelchair, helping me into the travel cart and getting me to my gate. But he then asked the next question *(What else can I do now?).* The answer to this question was actually two-fold. First, he stayed with me until my flight boarded, just in case my gate changed and second, he arranged for the airplane aisle chair to be brought to my gate.

The final piece of the **WOW** was that he asked and answered the third question *(What else can I do* later, *or* for *later?)*. He thought about what would happen when I arrived in Orlando and realized that if I was unable to walk in Chicago, I certainly would not be able to do so in Orlando, either. So, he called ahead to arrange for a wheelchair for me at the end of my long and exhausting trip.

By thinking ahead, proactively and compassionately on my behalf, of all the things I would need to complete my journey, even to the things I would need *after* I left his company, Victor created a **WOW** for me that will stay with me for as long as I live.

We can also create **WOW**s for our customers and co-workers by implementing the 1-2-3 formula. Although these questions and their answers vary from situation to situation, the concepts contained within them can be planned for ahead of time, in order to allow exceptional service and service recovery to occur as a normal part of doing business. Rather than being limited to certain situations (such as following a negative customer event) and certain groups of people (external customers), common scenarios can be brainstormed:

- ⊙ Ahead of time, in anticipation of group and individual interactions.
- ⊙ Every time an interaction between two groups or individuals occurs.
- ⊙ When positive and negative customer events occur.
- ⊙ With relation to internal and external customers alike.

Try this formula. It's quick, it's simple, and you never know who will benefit so much from their experience with you that your **WOW** will remain with them for the rest of their lives.

Combining the 1-2-3 Formula with the Target

Another way to use the templates is to combine the 1-2-3s of Doing More Than Appease to the target. Victor's story is applied in the following model to demonstrate this combination of concepts.

(Incidentally, the model for this case is further impacted by the fact that Victor was not the initially-assigned cart driver Airport Security called but who never arrived.)

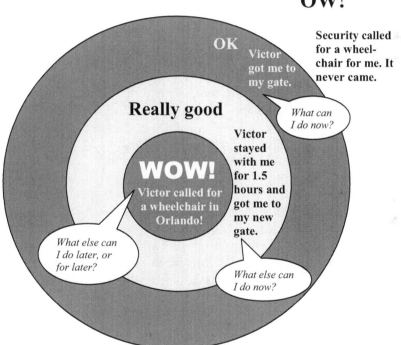

You Can be Human and Still Get Your Job Done

Case in Point:

   My husband has a friend named Joe, who is larger than life. Joe stands 6'5" tall, and is a big burly guy with a shock of white hair on his head and a completely infectious laugh that can be heard from one end of a room to the other. He absolutely loves life and it shows!

   Joe once had a job as a debt collector, which seems like a contradiction because I'm sure most of us don't know many debt collectors who seem like they really love life. But I believe Joe may have been the perfect person for this job because he is *human,* and too many debt collectors are *humanoids* who forget they are dealing with human beings while performing this challenging job. But Joe never forgot that he was dealing with people, rather than "accounts."

   He told us of a time when he went to the home a family who had gotten so far behind in making payments on their stove that it had to be repossessed. When Joe got there to take the stove, the woman of the house said, *"But dinner is cooking and it's not done yet!"* Any humanoid would have said, *"Too bad! Get the food off the stove. I'm taking it!"* But not Joe. Being *human,* he had gotten to know this family over the past several months. He liked them. More impressively, they liked *him*! So, the woman said, *"Why don't you stay for dinner? I'll finish cooking, we'll have dinner, and then you can take the stove. Will that be OK?"*

   So, Joe stayed for dinner, and when it was over, they put the food away and Joe took the stove when he left! On another occasion, Joe went to a house to repossess the TV, but when he got there, the children were watching cartoons. So, what do you think Joe did? You guessed it! He sat down and watched cartoons with the children for the next 15 minutes, and *then* took the TV.

I don't know about you, but I don't know many people who would invite their debt collector to dinner! For that matter, how many debt collectors do you know who are *human* enough to get invited to dinner, or be allowed to sit and interact with the children of their customers? Joe proves beautifully that no matter how challenging the job or the situation, you can be *human* and still get your job done.

The Bigger Picture

Another point to remember is that humanoids cannot appreciate context or nuance; humans can. If we focus solely on one small piece of the puzzle, we may miss the bigger picture in which it exists, as well as any nuances we can use to create a **WOW**.

A funny example of this occurred when Hurricane Charley came through the Orlando area in 2004. Around 11:00pm, after it had passed through, everyone began coming out of their homes to survey the damage. Several neighbors came to our home, and upon seeing our mangled screen door, one of them said, *"Holy cow! Look what happened to the Geroux's screen door,"* to which another neighbor replied, *"The Geroux's screen door? Look what happened to the Geroux's whole screen enclosure!"* The first neighbor had been so focused on the door

that he missed the fact that the corner containing the door was the *only* piece of the enclosure still left standing!

That is not to say that this neighbor is a humanoid; he's not. He is actually a good friend. He was simply exhibiting the kind of tunnel vision to which all humans fall prey at one time or another. Sometimes we are so surprised or shocked at an event, that we focus on the one shocking piece we notice first, and fail to see the rest of it until someone brings it to our attention. No humans can avoid experiencing this phenomenon on occasion.

The difference is that while all humans *occasionally* fall prey to this effect, it is *a way of life* for humanoids who simply do not have the resources or training to avoid using tunnel vision in their dealings with others. They are so focused on the task at hand that they miss the subtleties of the big picture, enabling them to effectively "power through" their jobs, while too often leaving a trail of steaming carcasses in their wake. This results in de-motivated and demoralized associates and co-workers who must deal with these co-workers.

Never Let 'Em Forget Their "Why"

One way of keeping humanity alive in the **WOWplace** and keeping your team connected emotionally to your goals is to always keep reminders in sight of why your team is performing their duties, and how they will help the organization accomplish its goals.

One way to achieve this is to post your mission, vision and values to remind everyone of what you stand for and strive to accomplish. Posting these reminders not only helps staff members focus on what's important, but also lets customers and other visitors know how committed you are to achieving them.

Case in Point:

I once went to a hospital for an X-ray. When I arrived at the X-ray Department, I was pleasantly surprised to see the X-ray Department Mission posted on the wall right next to the door. I can't tell you how good it made me feel as a patient to know that not only did the X-ray Department have a mission, but they posted it on the wall so patients could see it, and associates could be reminded of it at all times.

This simple act showed me that *humans* worked there, who remembered they were dealing with other humans in need of their medical services. It was one tiny action that cost the hospital virtually nothing (it was a piece of plain white paper taped to the door!), but it visibly proclaimed their humanity and caring.

What is your organization's mission? Is it understandable and memorable? Does everyone know it? If you asked your associates right now what your mission is, could they tell you? Better yet, could they tell you what it means? For the organization? For the customer? For them personally?

In addition, what is each department's mission? Do they all have individual departmental missions? How does that department's actions contribute to the success of the organization as a whole? How does it help customers? How do you let them know that what they do makes a difference?

Don't forget to re-visit these statements periodically to ensure they are currently still relevant. If they were written 50 years ago in language and terms that no longer apply, or if they are so long and convoluted that no one could possibly remember or understand them, it is time to update and simplify them so they are meaningful to your current organization and associates. Let them serve as guides regarding how associates should behave in order to accomplish the sentiment contained in those statements.

One way to achieve this is to post visible reminders of the good that has been done, past and present, to remind everyone of what you are all about. Using creative tools such as InfoGraphics to quickly allow everyone to see results to date, or other reminders (like the method used by many charities to "light up one floor of the Empire State Building for each $1,000 raised!"), or another fun way to track progress, can spur people on to higher results. A couple of examples of Infographics are below.

12,345 residents remained CONNECTED throughout the hurricane!

4,500 patients treated in 2012

Another way to keep the team connected to their "why" is to let them see the results and benefits of their combined efforts.

Case in Point:

I once read a case study of a children's museum whose international IT team was having difficulty creating cohesion and getting the job done. Most of them had never met, and each was focused on a different part of the IT solution, so they hadn't developed an emotional or personal connection to each other. The situation also made it difficult to see the big picture and how they fit together. Compounding the problem was the fact that their technologically-driven communication vehicles left much to be desired, as written words were misinterpreted, insult was taken where none was intended, and time lags caused other problems that well-connected teams do not experience.

To help ease the situation, organizational leaders brought the team together in the city where the museum existed. They also planned a team field trip to the museum so everyone could see the building and all its exhibits, and experience first-hand the joy and wonder on the faces of the children who visited.

Afterward, they engaged in team-building exercises to help team members get to know each other better, as well as an informal dinner where team members talked about anything *but* work, in order to get to know each other as fellow *humans*, rather than simply as co-workers.

The result was astonishing! Rather than focusing just on their individual pieces of the work, which when considered independently of the project meant nothing to them, the team was subsequently able to focus on the end result of their work together.

By reinforcing the emotional connection, humanizing the team and helping them remember *why* they were doing what they were doing, leaders helped the team become more connected and more productive as a result.

Dangerous Mindsets to Watch for and Thoughts to Overcome Them

"I'm not their Mom or Dad. Just let me do my job. Why do I have to worry about their emotions and feelings?"

Being kind and considerate of other people's feelings is not the sole domain of "Mom" and "Dad."It is the domain of every human on the planet. We do not have to "worry" about other people's feelings, and we may not be responsible for the way they react to events that occur. But if we want to be successful, compassionate and *human*, we *do* have to at least consider other people's feelings, rather than just trampling over them because we refuse to consider the impact of our actions on others.

"No one ever worried about my emotions, and I'm just fine!"

Just because no one ever worried about treating you with kindness does not justify continuing that pattern. This line of thinking follows the traditional cycle of abuse and poverty, and is one of the main reasons why abuse and poverty are perpetuated from generation to generation. No one ever did it for them (in other words, no one ever showed them another way), so they just do what they know. But that does not mean it's the only – or even the best – way to handle a situation. Following a cycle of being inconsiderate of other people's feelings only creates increasingly more situations where humans feel undervalued, resentful, and disengaged. Teamwork, productivity, and effectiveness all suffer as a result.

"There is no place for emotions in the workplace."

Too late! Emotions are already in the workplace. Unfortunately, much of it is negative, as leaders battle petty arguments, jealousy, and negative attitudes every day. It is time to invite positive emotion into the workplace to counteract – and possibly avoid – the negative emotion that enters uninvited. If we are forced to deal with negative emotion in the workplace anyway, we must proactively introduce some positive emotion there as well, in an effort to prevent the *only* experience our associates have with emotion in the workplace being those on the negative side.

In addition, do not make the mistake of equating emotion with loss of control. This was the mistake of Vulcans like Mr. Spock, who felt that because emotions were often uncontrollable, they had to eliminate all of them, including the positive ones. There is no place for un-bridled or unrestrained emotion in the workplace. But emotion can be controlled. It also has a positive side that absolutely has a place in the workplace. It comes in many forms, including consideration, respect, courtesy and compassion. If we eliminate all forms of emotion, unfortunately the good ones go out with the bad. Let's not "throw the baby out with the bath water." Rather, let's figure out which emotions have a positive place, not only in society, but in our workplaces as well, and tap into the engaging power it offers to our teams.

*How to **WOW** By Being More Human*

1. **Show you care.** Ask questions or make occasional comments of personal interest in others as human beings, not just as associates. Do the unexpected: ask about someone's day, or an upcoming event in their life. Pay them a little personal attention. And lest you think, *"I'm too busy; I don't have time to stop and ask them about trivial things,"* I'd like to point out:

   ⊙ The very fact that you are a leader and very busy is what makes *any* amount of personal attention from you even more significant. The higher your level in the company, the more relevant this is. The mere fact that you *know* a pertinent fact about an associate's life, and then take the time to ask about it, means more to them than it would coming from a peer because a) they know how difficult it is for you to take the time to do it, and b) most leaders don't do it, making you exceptional for even trying.

⊙ Even though little things may seem trivial to you, they are definitely not trivial to them. The fact that they are "trivial" when compared to everything else you must think about on the job is what *makes* them meaningful. Besides, although they are trivial, they are not easy to do. If they were easy, they wouldn't mean as much because *everyone* would do it.

Case in Point:

I currently serve as a consultant to a large company. One day, the CEO and I had scheduled a conference call. At the end of the call, rather than simply hanging up when our business was concluded, he asked me about an upcoming speaking engagement. After I told him when it was, he wished me good luck, then added, *"I know you'll knock it out of the park!"*

WOW! All it took was 30 seconds, but he made me feel like a million bucks! Just the fact that he remembered I had that engagement, and then took his valuable time on the call to say something before hanging up, showed me his "true colors," and that he doesn't just talk a good game, he *walks* his talk. I've seen many examples of this throughout my dealings with him. He is respectful and *human* to everyone on (and off) his team, at every level of the company – and everyone loves him for it.

⊙ Malcolm Gladwell's book Blink! points out that it does not take a lot of time to do something exceptional. In one example, he compared medical professionals who had been sued for malpractice with those who had not. Doctors who spent an average of only 3.3 minutes longer with each patient (on a

15-18 minute average visit) tended not to be sued for malpractice. Obviously, this was one of several differentiating factors between the two groups, but it was a noticeable pattern in the study. You don't have to – and can't – take a lot of time doing this, but the key is not to appear rushed. Don't do it if you can't do it properly, but when the opportunity arises, take 30 seconds and do something nice.

2. **Watch for contradictions and inadvertent messages in your actions.** Be careful that your actions do not contradict your words when you verbalize, for example, that you don't think you are above anyone else in your company, or that any company task is beneath you. Do not, for example, walk by a piece of trash on the floor without picking it up. And do not *always* delegate getting coffee. Surprise your assistant once in a while and ask if *she'd* like a cup of coffee while you are going to get your own. Create little surprises as convenient opportunities arise to **WOW** your associates with actions that show you "walk your talk."

3. **Model the behavior you wish to see in others.** Make eye contact, smile, keep your eyes up and look around as you walk through the halls. What happens when others are looking down or away and you look at them, smile, and say *"Hi?"* They usually reciprocate by raising their eyes, smiling, and saying *"Hi"* back. Think also of how the other person reacts in a confrontation. If you allow yourself to get upset, they get even *more* upset. But if you keep negative emotions in check and display compassion, courtesy, and respect, they usually calm down and respond in kind. By modeling the behavior you wish to see, you inspire others to reflect that behavior back to you. If

they don't, you can still hold your head high and know you acted with dignity, despite what the other person did.

4. **Create and maintain a focus on Human Duties.** Look at your job postings. Who are you trying to recruit? Ensure getting the right candidates by listing not only the required *job* skills, but the desired *human* skills and attitudes, as well. Conversely, if you are a candidate, look for postings that mention these attitudes and a service focus, rather than just technical abilities. List these qualities in your resume, skills portfolio, cover letter and job applications. Convey the fact that you are human. Create and post a personal mission statement.

   ◉ Introduce a "Human Duties" category to your organization's efforts and goals.

   ◉ Add them to job postings to let people know what is expected of them in this regard, right from the start . . . before they are even hired!

   ◉ Add this category for measurement on performance reviews and include not only technical performance, but also desired attributes, attitudes and values.

   ◉ Add it to associate Individual Development Plans (IDPs) to demonstrate how these characteristics will help associates in their career development.

5. **Review your organizational Mission, Vision, Values and Purpose Statements.** Re-write them if necessary! What are you *really* trying to say? *Do* they and *can* they connect with human emotions?

   ◉ Share mission statements with all associates. No one is at too low a level to be told the mission of the company. Entry-level workers are usually the ones directly interacting with customers on the front lines. Yet mission statements are too often the "domain" of the executives of the company, stockholders and websites, but not directly expressed and reinforced as part of the company culture shared with all employees upon being hired or interviewed.

Case in Point:

Early in my working career, I worked for five different companies where I was never told the mission.

At the beginning, I was unaware that mission statements even existed because I was too new to the working world! Once I saw them (on an Annual Report to stockholders), I thought, *"Oh, that's what we're all about!"* What a way for someone to find out what they are working to accomplish.

◉ Post mission statements everywhere: work areas, public areas, websites, blogs, newsletters, FaceBook, Twitter and other social media sites. If you are going to take the time and effort to be human, show it; don't hide it in a folder, or bury it in an Annual Report so only stockholders can see it, but customers and associates never know what they are.

◉ Keep reinforcing the mission statements; don't share them once, then let everyone forget them. Put them everywhere! Create posters for the work areas. Put them on business cards, screen savers, associate newsletters. Reinforce them verbally in meetings and other gatherings. Do not allow the type of "situational blindness" that enables everyone to walk right by them and act in a manner that contradicts them, even though they're in plain sight, but have been forgotten.

◉ NOTE: If you post any statements or customer promises, ensure that all associates act according to them, or a big disconnect will result that could turn off customers even more than if you had never posted them.

> **Case in Point:**
>
> I remember a store that advertised *"If we see three people in line, we'll open another register!"* Customers were thrilled to see these posters!
>
> However, store managers were held to such unforgiving profit margins that they couldn't properly staff their stores to keep this promise. Hence, when customers in long lines did not see more registers opening to accommodate them, they rebelled en masse, with many of them abandoning full shopping carts out of sheer disgust and frustration!

6. **Review your organizational policies.** Do our policies and procedures demonstrate our human values? Do our scripts and other communications outline them and guide our behavior and our words to create **WOW**s? When we say we offer customer rewards, do we put unreasonable limitations on them that make customers feel de-valued rather than valued more? Are they really rewards if we never allow customers to use them? Do our words match our actions? Do we *cheerfully* refund customers' money if they are dissatisfied and try to use our "Money-Back Guarantee?" Are there "loopholes" that prevent them from using the guarantee? Are we creating **WOW**s with our words, only to create even bigger OWs with our subsequent actions?

7. **Create policies that focus on "Human Duties."** Create a policy that guides associates' daily actions and attitudes. Sample Policy: *"We will never ignore anyone in our immediate vicinity."*
   Sample Explanation: We will scan our immediate area when in public locations, and never ignore any associate or visitor in that area. We will nod, smile or wave if the person is engaged in a conversation, so as not to interrupt that conversation. If the person is alone, we will speak to them, at least to say, *"Hello."*

If the person is a visitor or looks like they could use help, we will offer it.

One Final Note: Expect Human Duties Up Front

This chapter has so far focused mainly on how to recognize and remember our human duties while working. However, as noted in a couple of areas, if we let people know up front that we expect them to perform according to our values and exhibit a focus on human duties, it can make all the difference in the world because they know what they are getting into up front. Those who connect with that philosophy will stay on and perform. Those who don't will not even make it to the workplace.

The following article about an exceptional company, Zappos, places special emphasis on the human elements of doing our jobs well. While there is a ton of great information in here about being human, the big focus I would like to point out for this story, however, is the first revealing aspect of Zappos. Take a look at how they emphasize who they want to hire, and how they allow new hires to "self-select" out of the company if they do not fit company values.

The secret weapon of Zappos: patience

(This information is proudly provided by *Business Management Daily.com*: http://www.businessmanagementdaily.com/26886/the secret -weapon-of-zappos-patience)

Online shoe retailer Zappos has gotten a lot of attention for its knockout customer service.

But Tony Hsieh (pronounced "Shay"), founder of the billion-dollar company, says his secret of success is really about his associates.

"The No. 1 focus and priority for the company, even though we want the brand to be about customer service, is company culture," he

says. *"Our belief is that if you get the culture right, most of the other stuff, like great customer service, will just happen."*

What is behind his thinking: Because organizations are now so transparent – anything they do, good or bad, can be reported instantly on the web – it is more important than ever to run a harmonious workplace.

Two revealing aspects of Zappos:

1. All hires receive five weeks of training at company headquarters in Las Vegas (associates speak, unscripted, with customers). After the first week, every trainee gets a choice between staying with the firm, or taking $2,000 plus expenses to leave. Those who stay (over 97%) can brag that they passed up an easy two grand to work at Zappos.

2. Associates go beyond filling orders. A woman called saying she was having trouble locating a specific type of boot for her husband. Zappos shipped them overnight. Days later, the customer called back: Her husband had been killed in a car accident and she needed help returning the boots. The call center agent not only took care of the return, but sent flowers as well.

Hsieh encourages associates to put a human face on the company, engage with customers and share "behind the scene stuff" via social media. *"Your culture and your brand are two sides of the same coin,"* he says. A typical Hsieh tweet to his 1,950,000 followers lauds great customer service: (from the airport in Austin, Texas) *"TSA guy giving a genuine, specific compliment to each person after passing through the metal detector. **WOW**."*

Asked why more organizations aren't like Zappos, he offers one word: "Patience." Most firms, Hsieh says, won't put in the time to build employee morale and customer service. *"It's whether you're willing to make that commitment."*

Adapted from "Zappos CEO Tony Hsieh," *Knowledge@W.P. Carey*, http://knowledge.wpcarey.asu.edu.

Now, *that's* the way to get people who really connect with your human values to work with you!

Chapter Summary:
How to WOW Through Making the WOWplace Human

1. Be human . . . not humanoid.
2. Job duties vs. human duties.
3. Human leaders create **WOW**s.
4. A little humility goes a long way.
5. The seemingly paradoxical benefit of being human in a leadership position.
6. The promotion phenomenon.
7. Arrogance vs. confidence.
8. **WOW**ers act according to their values (a.k.a. the story of Victor's Values).
9. The importance of proactive thinking in creating the **WOW**.
10. The 1-2-3s of doing more than appease.
    a. What can I do now?
    b. What else can I do now?
    c. What can I do later . . . or for later?
11. Applying the 1-2-3 formula to Victor's Values.
12. Combining the 1-2-3 formula with the target.
13. You can be human and still get your job done.
14. The bigger picture.
15. Never let 'em forget their "why."
16. Dangerous mindsets to watch for, and thoughts to overcome them.
17. How to **WOW** by being more human.
18. One final note: expect human duties up front.
19. The secret weapon of Zappos: patience.

Chapter Six:

WOWplace Rule #4

A **WOWplace** is Innovative,

Creative and Fun!

A **WOWplace** is Innovative, Creative and Fun!

No organization is standing still; no organization can afford to do so. Innovation, creativity and fun are absolute requirements in the **WOWplace**, where associates are constantly creating new ways to get better at producing quality products and services, providing **WOW** experiences to customers and associates and making a positive difference in their world.

This means they have to constantly resist the status quo in order to ensure that innovation, creativity and fun become an integral part of their culture. It also means focusing on what people can do – not what they can't do – to make things better and easier for associates and customers.

Innovation for the sake of innovation alone is not usually a good enough reason to do it. Of course, there are times when we just want to do something new and different, something unique. But most of the time when we are asked to focus on what we *can* do, it is because we really *should* do it. Either customers are asking for it, or it is just the right thing to do. In other words, there is a solid business reason for doing it. Innovation with a purpose helps us, among other things:

- Create new products and services.
- Improve existing products and services.
- Find ways to increase profits by saving money or reducing costs.
- Improve processes, which increases accuracy, reliability, productivity and service.
- Keep ordinary tasks fresh.
- Obtain and use new knowledge.
- Find ways to WOW customers and co-workers.

All of this helps us create a competitive advantage by differentiating us from our competition.

Allowing for innovation and creativity also helps us put the fun and excitement back into our jobs. It is much more exciting for associates to work at a company that's innovating and growing, rather than one that's stagnating or struggling. We all want to feel that we are making a difference. And when we are allowed to use our creativity to do so, it makes a world of difference with regard to how engaged we are.

Give Associates Some Sense of Influence and Control

We all know that people are generally much more engaged at home or in their community than at their workplace. Besides the fact that these environments are much more fun and connected to us personally, why else is this the case? It is because these are the places where people usually feel they have a much greater sense of control and impact than they do in the workplace.

Workplaces are more structured and controlled out of necessity. However, if a workplace is so excessively rigid as to disallow any free thought or expression of new ideas, or it discourages anyone from acting on them, workers begin to feel a sense of uselessness and powerlessness, and eventually stop trying. No one can be motivated to make a difference if they don't even feel they have the slightest bit of control over their own destiny, or if they believe they have no positive impact on their environment.

There are many ways to provide associates with a sense of control. One common way is to allow for flexible hours wherever possible. As life becomes more and more complicated and crammed with various obligations and commitments that must be met during the workday, associates find it increasingly difficult to juggle work with other responsibilities. Having flexibility in at least one area of their life makes it easier for them to concentrate on what needs to be done, remain less stressed over competing priorities, and accomplish all they need to do.

A second way to help associates feel a greater sense of control is to ensure that your expectations of them are clearly communicated, and that they possess the tools, knowledge and support to accomplish them. There is no greater sense of accomplishment than when some-one has a goal, feels empowered to achieve it, and then gets the job done. But there is no greater sense of frustration than having someone say they expect something from you without giving you the specific goals, details, tools or support to carry it out.

Lay out your goals and expectations, including timeframes, benchmarks, metrics, and other measures to let associates know exact-ly what the goal is, measure their progress toward it, and realize when they have reached it. Don't forget to reward them all along the way (this is especially important if the goal or project is large or long term) and then again at the end of the process. By rewarding each segment of the goal as it is completed, associates are reminded of, as well as rewarded for, the goals they are expected to be focused on achieving. We'll talk more about rewards in the next chapter, but we must not forget this all-important piece of the motivation puzzle.

Another method of empowering associates is to help them save time and money by providing extra amenities at the work site that they would otherwise have to travel elsewhere to find. For example, at the Googleplex campus in Mountain View, CA, associates can enjoy free meals, exercise at the gym, get a haircut, get their dry cleaning done, enjoy lots of sunlight, work in creative and collaborative spaces, play games, take a nap and even play the piano. The halls of this **WOW-place** are also filled with whiteboards where ideas can be openly shared. By providing so many different services at the work site, Google associates are encouraged to stay on campus for longer periods of time, which also makes them more productive. Paradoxically, associates don't resent staying there because doing so eases their time and budgetary constraints, creating a mutually productive situation! Google's hope is that the associated increases in collaboration, creativity and productivity will enable their associates to envision Google's next great product or service.

Of course, not every company can afford to provide all of the amenities that Google provides. But every company can permit associates to think of ways to make their work spaces look different and feel more customized. For example, most companies allow associates to customize their personal workspace. But several companies have taken it a step further by allowing associates to decorate their common break room. One company's associates decorated the break room like a movie theater, with movie posters on the walls, a snack bar, and even a popcorn machine. Another allowed associates to have a mural of a beach painted on one wall, and provided lounge chairs for them to lie on while taking their breaks.

Conduct a survey, or appoint a committee to find out what associates would like to do. Give them a budget, and let them decide how they might like to make their work environment more enjoyable.

The important point is that a **WOWplace** looks, sounds and feels different from an ordinary workplace. So, get to know your associates and what they like, and offer them choices that help them feel as though they have a little more control over their environment, their work and their own success.

Where do people want to live and work? Not in "caves" or "rabbit warrens" with blank, empty walls. Not cut off from everyone and everything they care about. They want to collaborate, so wherever possible – and within budget and guidelines – let them collaboratively design their shared spaces such as break rooms, meeting rooms and cafeterias, as well as individual spaces such as their cubicles, offices and desks.

It is not always easy to strike the right balance when trying to please many associates. But it is definitely worth putting some resources into brainstorming and empowering them with choices *they* can select in various areas, rather than forcing them to live with just one choice in *every* area, none of which they have had any input in implementing.

Providing the tangible benefits that associates seek is an effective way to get them engaged. But more importantly, we must focus on the *intangible* atmosphere that either sets the stage for creativity and innovation, or stifles it. It is crucial that we let people know it's OK to be creative by making it *safe* for them to do so (as delineated in **WOWplace** Rule #1). However, we must go further than simply making it safe for workers to innovate and have fun; we must also set the stage for them to effectively "think outside the box."

To Think Outside *the Box, There Has to* be *a Box!*

Creative brainstorming is a key tool for encouraging collaboration and cooperation in the **WOWplace**. For many years we have all been told that in order to come up with solutions, we must think outside the box. But to effectively think outside the box, there must *be* a clearly defined box. And that is where we have to begin: *inside* the box.

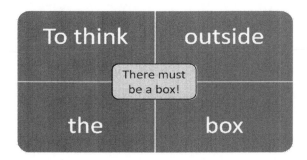

We often ask people to be creative, throwing challenges at them without giving them enough structure to even begin the process effectively. They don't have a clear starting point or understandable goals and objectives. There is no benchmark, no metrics, and no way to create "steps" so progress can be planned and incrementally achieved. For these reasons, they fail to come up with anything useful because they are not provided enough information to succeed. No one can create in a vacuum. Consequently, many won't even try.

The most effective way to produce real change and help people succeed is to follow the advice of the well-known African proverb, *"Eat the elephant one bite at a time."* Hence, the need for the box representing the structure, the essential common starting point and that all-important first "bite."

The box represents the structure, the clear starting point

The box could represent the average experience provided by those in your industry. If so, the first step is to look inside the box and identify what everyone else is doing. If they are not doing it well, being outside the box indicates what you are willing and able to do that they cannot – or will not – do. If they *are* doing it well, being outside the box means finding ways to do it bigger and better, or being more relevant and valuable for others including customers, associates and the community. The box could also represent a negative experience that needs to be changed or a problem to be solved within your organization, in which case the box represents your current situation.

For example, what if a company needed to save money? Simply telling associates that they need to "save money" is too vague a goal to actually achieve. Since there are so many possible ways the company could be wasting money, they don't even know where to begin to look. Even if they do know where to look, with no specific goal in mind, how do they know how *much* money to save? What is the magnitude of the problem? Where does the biggest problem exist? Where have improvements already been made, so previous efforts are not duplicated?

These types of questions represent the structure and clarity provided by the "box." Once the box is known, then we can think outside it to improve the situation, one actionable and measurable step at a time.

So, start with the basics to ensure everyone is on the same page:

◉ **Establish a distinct starting point.** This includes a clear statement of the problem and any current solutions – even incomplete attempts or workarounds. If possible, provide examples of similar problems and what others did to solve them.

◉ **Determine and communicate clear objectives.** Does everyone know them? Does everyone understand them? What does the end goal look like?

◉ **Provide tools and support systems.** People must be provided the proper tools and support systems to accomplish the goals that enable their success. For example, in the popular film, Apollo 13, engineers were given a problem to solve: they had to make the round end of one tube fit into the square end of another in order to get more oxygen to the astronauts. So, they took duplicates of everything that the astronauts had to work with, laid it all out on the table in the pile, showed the square piece and the round piece, and said, "We have to make this fit into the hole for this (pointing to the round and square pieces), using nothing but that (indicating the parts on the table)." By showing them exactly what the end result needed to look like, as well as every tool available at their disposal, they made the "impossible" task possible.

◉ **Identify roles, responsibilities and deadlines.** Who will do what, and by when? Who is responsible, and who will serve as support? A wise old tale illustrates the importance of this point. It is the story of four people: everyone, no one, anyone and someone. There was a job to be done. Anyone could have done it. Everyone thought someone would do it, but no one did it. Therefore, the job didn't get done! Don't allow your roles and responsibilities to be so poorly defined that no one knows who is responsible for doing what, and when.

◉ **Have measures and reporting mechanisms, as well as recognition and reward systems in place to encourage associates to participate fully.** (I will talk more about the importance and impact of recognition and reward systems in the next chapter.)

With all of the things we *must* do listed above, there is one thing we must *not* do: micromanage. If the proper team is in place, there is no need to look over their shoulder every second and dictate *how* they must accomplish every aspect or step of their goals. There are times when the exact process is unknown, and trying to dictate a "known" solution could sabotage the efforts of the team. Obviously, leaders need to stay involved and informed, and the team must be guided and held accountable. But determine the appropriate level of involvement for the team and the leader and use it to encourage, inspire, empower and engage the team, rather than de-valuing the team's input, stifling their creativity and slowing their momentum by micromanaging them.

Breaking the Norm and Challenging the Status Quo

The only way companies continue to innovate is by challenging the status quo. **WOW**ers look at common situations and requests, and instead of seeing excuses to be ordinary, see them as ways to differentiate themselves and gain a competitive advantage by doing what their competitors are not willing to do. They are not afraid to question the status quo. Instead, they think about what situations and requests have arisen where excuses are used instead of creative thinking and ask, *"Does it have to be this way?"*

Are you moving forward, or simply marking time and stagnating in your industry? How do you answer the following questions?

- ◉ What is the normal experience for customers and associates in our industry? How does ours compare?
- ◉ Do we succumb to the temptation to do the "average," assuming that "everyone else does it, so we can, too?" Or that "no one else does it, so why should we go to that trouble?"
- ◉ Do we dismiss new ideas without real consideration if they appear too different, too hard or too "crazy" to try to implement?

Depending on your answers to these questions, you may need to challenge yourself and your team to do things differently than you've ever done them before, to rise above and create an experience that is so far superior to your competition that it **WOW**s customers and associates alike.

Again, this goes back to creating an atmosphere that is safe for associates to take reasonable and appropriate risks. If done properly, these actions have the capacity to carry you farther than your competition could dream of going, both in terms of getting and keeping new customers, and getting and retaining exceptional associates.

Let's look at some principles for challenging the status quo and getting associates to think imaginatively to create **WOW** experiences.

Issue a Bold *Challenge*

Don't you love a challenge? Where is the satisfaction and thrill if there is no challenge in anything? Isn't the pride and satisfaction of solving a difficult challenge more fulfilling and rewarding than that of accomplishing easy tasks? Obviously, we all need a few easy tasks thrown into the mix once in a while so we don't become overly frustrated with never-ending difficulties. But an occasional bold challenge with a noble purpose can galvanize a team, especially when team members are connected with and committed to their leader's goals. It has been proven that letting associates know that the company needs help during challenging times can stimulate them to reach unprecedented heights, because it gives them a reason to come together for a common goal, such as keeping the company alive, saving their jobs, or helping customers solve big problems.

That's because it is in these situations that associates can more clearly see the direct impact of their actions on a specific goal. If, for example, a company is ready to fold and associates come together to develop and execute a good plan to keep it from doing so – and then succeed – the impact of their actions is clearly visible, relatable to the goal and measurable. In other words, it follows the formula set forth in this chapter regarding how to ensure that everyone is operating under the same principles:

- There is a clear starting point (e.g., the company is ready to fold).
- There are clear objectives (e.g., we need to generate $xxx, xxx dollars in sales in the next 60 days).
- Roles, responsibilities and deadlines are established (i.e., everyone knows what they must personally do to help achieve the goal and how their actions contribute to everyone's success).
- Measures are in place to monitor and report progress.
- Everyone is probably too busy performing their own duties to micromanage anyone else.

In this scenario, everyone is empowered to do their best to create the desired results. When the goal is accomplished, everyone gets to celebrate, mainly by retaining their jobs, but also by participating in a joint acknowledgment of pride, respect and admiration for the job they did together!

This type of situation also reinforces the importance of never letting associates forget their "why," which we discussed in Chapter Five. The "why" is so important and crucial that they absolutely can't forget it. Thus, they remained focused on the goals because they know why they are doing their assigned tasks, they've been given the power, authority and ability to carry them out, and they see the direct impact of their actions on the status of that "why."

Be Willing to Do the Extraordinary Despite Every Excuse Not To

The concept above of issuing a bold challenge can bring out the best in everyone and inspire them to do the seemingly impossible. But when we look at those situations closely, are they really impossible, or just difficult or extraordinary? Are we calling the difficult "impossible" because we have dismissed the idea before even investigating whether or not it can be done?

The following is an example of an organization that questioned the status quo and created a huge **WOW** by being willing to do what most companies in their industry were unwilling to do.

Case in Point:

My husband and I have had body work done on our cars at Universal Auto Body in Orlando. We found this establishment through our car insurance company, which recommended them because they do great work there and never gouge their customers.

That was a nice enough surprise, but the *real* surprise was what we saw when we got there. The grounds were neat and clean, and we were greeted by a man dressed in a nice pair of pants and clean shirt, not by someone in a dirty, greasy jumpsuit. He determined the work we wanted done, told us their process, brought us to the lobby to wait for our car, and then took the car to the work area.

Another nice surprise waited inside for us. The lobby was spacious, neat, clean and quiet. There were comfy chairs, tables, a coffee station, and even artwork on the walls. What was absent was the dirt, grease and noise ever-present in other body shops.

When our car was done, the same well-dressed man came back to get us, brought the car around to show us the work and get our approval, helped us with the paperwork and sent us on our way. The estimate was right on target and the work was top-notch.

It's been this way every time we've been there. In fact, one time we mentioned to the receptionist how impressed we were with the place, and she was so proud of it herself that she offered to give us a tour of the shop. Even the work areas were immaculate! We never would have believed it possible if we hadn't seen it for ourselves.

How could anyone get people excited about something as difficult and unusual as cleaning and "classing up" an auto body shop? First, remember that what seems mundane to one person is actually thrilling to someone else! Therefore, it is crucial that, as often as possible, we hire people who are excited by the same things as we are (not necessarily taking pride in cleaning up a body shop – but taking pride in the appearance of *wherever* they work). Second, by instilling such a sense of pride in accomplishing not only what is expected, but what other body shops proclaim is practically impossible – neatness, cleanliness, even elegance – we spur all team members on with the challenge alone!

The "impossible" is only impossible until someone comes along and says it isn't. Actually, it is really not about doing the impossible; it's about doing the unexpected. This company had every reason *not* to do what they did because no customer expected them to do it. In fact, most people probably never even thought of it, or would have thought it could be done. But by taking on that challenge and actually doing it, they created a **WOW**, which in turn generates tons of word-of-mouth advertising for them. I have recommended them to countless individuals because of their superb service, excellent work, reasonable prices and the **WOW** way they conduct business at their organization. You can get any one of the other pieces alone in many body shops, but the **WOW** is in the fact that all of them exist in the same place.

The following is one more example of something that seemed impossible, but was proven to be not only possible, but immensely successful, because an "impossible" idea wasn't just slammed down.

Case in Point:

The job of a hotel concierge may seem like it must be in person at the hotel. However, as reported by *NBC News*, the exceptional concierge at the Hyatt Regency Santa Clara, Anna Mariano-Morris, is a teleworker! Several years ago her boss approved her to work from home so she could spend more time with her family and avoid a 1½-hour commute. Management paid to set up a webcam on her home computer, ran a T1 line to her home and put a 42-inch plasma TV with a webcam in the hotel lobby so she and hotel guests could see each other. She can converse with them, look up restaurants and local attractions online and remotely print out directions for guests at the hotel location. They call her "Virtual Anna" and the arrangement has been a great success.

Get Rid of the Excuses

All too often, innovative ideas are slammed down with the same old excuses. Statements such as, *"That's the way it's always been done!"* or *"We've never done that before!"* or *"No one else does it"* or *"Everyone else does it"* abound in many organizations, causing associates to shy away from doing anything other than what is common or easy. But the fact that everyone else – or no one else – does it is exactly why we should do the opposite! After all, do we really want to be ordinary? Commonplace? Average? Just like everyone else? Just because something has always been done a certain way, does that mean that's the way it will always be done? It can never change?

A **WOWplace** does not allow excuses to justify mediocrity or stagnation. We bring "new blood" into the organization for many reasons, not the least of which is to keep the company and its ideas and methodologies fresh. Therefore, we need to get rid of excuses that hold us back from creating **WOW**s in our organization! Excuses are so insidious that we sometimes can't recognize them because we are too close to the situation.

Case in Point:

I once heard a real estate professional utter the following sentence: *"I'm not making any money right now, but that's just because I hate my broker so much that I refuse to put another penny in his pocket!"*

Really? Doesn't he realize who else's pocket he's not putting another penny into with this type of behavior?

Instead of taking positive action to change an undesirable situation, this agent allowed this excuse to stop him from earning a living for himself and his family! Maybe what he was doing wasn't working to generate sales, or maybe he hated his broker and was de-motivated. Either way, a more productive action would have been to get rid of the excuses, find a new broker, get back to work and make some money!

Case in Point:

After putting an ad in a newspaper for a receptionist and scheduling a dozen appointments, I got a call from a young man who asked if the position was filled. When I told him it wasn't, but that I wasn't scheduling any more interviews, he said, *"Oh, please give me a chance! I'm a really good person and a hard worker. Please give me an interview – you won't be sorry!"*

WOW! I was so impressed by his earnestness that I agreed to give him an interview that afternoon, which would be our only opportunity to meet, since I would be going out of town the following day. However, after literally begging me to give him an interview, when I offered him the appointment, he said, *"But it's raining outside!"* Did I hear that correctly? I asked him, *"Does that mean that if I hire you and it rains some day, you won't be coming to work?"*

Obviously, it was "interview over" at that point. But this young man was too close to the situation (or maybe just a little too young) to realize he sabotaged himself with his attitudes and behavior.

These are just a couple of the many examples of how individuals sabotage their own personal success by using excuses they don't even recognize. This happens in organizations as well, since they are all made up of individuals who are susceptible to using these same types of excuses in their personal lives and bring that susceptibility to work.

WOWers get rid of the excuses holding them back and do the extraordinary, despite every reason not to do so, even when it would be easier to say, *"No one else does that, so why should we?"* Have your team members periodically do a check of their attitudes to be sure they are not falling back on the same old excuses whenever new ideas are proposed.

Be Flexible

Sometimes we come to a given situation with certain expectations, which may or may not be reasonable. Many times in my own life, I've discovered to my dismay that things do not always go as expected. I'm sure this has happened to you once or twice in your life. However, I've also discovered that if I am flexible enough to adapt to whatever happens, I can usually turn it into something positive, and often I discover that it was to my benefit that what I originally wished would happen, didn't!

Let's face it, few things happen as we expect! So, we can choose to be inflexible and complain and moan about it *not* happening as expected, or realize that if we can't change the situation, we must be flexible and creative enough to change our *expectations* in an effort to leverage them to our advantage.

Case in Point:

I spoke at a conference with over 12,000 attendees, as well as a trade show with more than 350 booths. This trade show was like no other I have ever attended. It was enormous and reminiscent of a circus, with many booths containing games, videos, giveaways, drawings and other interactive features designed to draw visitors. In fact, many people visit booths just for the giveaways and games. However, if they wanted to participate in the drawings, they had to allow the vendor to scan their badge and capture their contact information for lead follow-up. Sounds fair, right?

At lunch one day, an attendee sat down and said, *"You won't believe what just happened to me!"* She had visited a booth where the representative asked snidely, *"Are you interested in our services, or are you just here for the freebie?"* She was shocked! She told him she wasn't quite ready now, but may be interested in the future. But at lunch she told us she probably wouldn't use them because her experience with him had been so nasty and embarrassing.

OW! What happened there? The attendee had never heard of this company before, yet her first and only experience with them was such an OW that it defeated their whole purpose for being there, which should have been to establish relationships and set the stage for future follow-up, not sell attendees on their services right then! After all, did he really think he was going to make a sale at a circus?

His company paid a lot of money to be at that trade show, but his inflexibility once he was surprised by a situation that was different than he expected it to be, combined with his inability to readjust his expectations accordingly, actually destroyed opportunities to connect rather than creating them.

So, don't close off your options. Remember that situations are rarely what we expect them to be, and if you can't change the situation, change your expectations in order to capitalize

If you can't change your situation, change your expectations.

151

on new or unexpected opportunities as they arise. Don't eliminate options just because you didn't expect the current situation to occur.

Be Transparent

The transparency of at least admitting that there are issues needing to be addressed demonstrates a willingness to be as honest and up front as possible with associates, something often sorely lacking in the corporate environment. Associates know when something is wrong. We can either let them know the true depth of the real story or we can allow them to fill in the blanks, bolster the gossip grapevine – usually with incorrect information – and create even more problems due to inaccuracies in their information and the obvious unwillingness of executive management to trust associates with the truth.

This means balancing the truth with action plans and realistic appraisals of the situation. Associates need reassurance that their leader has a reasonable plan, can communicate it well, and has confidence that the plan will enable the company to achieve its goals.

Another way of achieving transparency is to be financially transparent. This includes not only as much corporate transparency as possible, but educating associates on how the company makes money, how the numbers work and how their actions help contribute to the success of the company. Associates will be more committed to doing the things that will contribute to the company's – and their own – financial success if they have a better understanding of how it works. Many associates have never been entrepreneurs or businesspeople. They may never have thought of the cause-and-effect of not taking the appropriate actions to drive the sales and income that make it possible to give them paychecks. If we don't sell, we can't pay associates; if we don't serve, we can't sell. If we waste money, it doesn't matter if we sell, we won't earn a profit. These basics are factors that many people have never considered, nor have they considered how their actions *affect* those basics and consequently, themselves.

In addition, being transparent and asking for help from associates lets them know their contributions, input and new ideas are valued, and that leaders are willing to listen to them and take their advice if workable solutions are presented.

Encourage Collaboration as Much as Possible

Whenever a unique or unusual challenge presents itself, especially a big one, collaboration is key because it Increases the creativity of any team. You must have noticed that creative juices flow better in a group, where ideas can bounce around from one person to another. It does not matter if the idea is a good one or not; every idea plays off another to create even more ideas. What one person doesn't think of, another does!

Therefore, collaboration is a key ingredient for success. People will reactively collaborate when a problem needs to be solved, but one way to turn your workplace into a **WOWplace** is to assemble a proactive **WOW** Team that holds periodic creativity meetings centered around a purpose or theme. The team could choose one specific area, process or task per meeting, and brainstorm ways to go from OW to **WOW** in that area before a big problem occurs or a customer complains about it.

Create a WOW Team to hold creativity meetings with a purpose or theme.

One meeting might be dedicated to brainstorming ways to make the lobby area more attractive or interesting in an effort to improve the visitor experience. (Even if it is currently presentable, how can we make it a **WOW**?)

Another meeting could be used to brainstorm how to make the associate on-boarding experience more of a **WOW**. For example, most of a new associate's workday is planned, but what is often overlooked is their free time, such as lunch or breaks. This can leave them on their own, feeling awkward about inviting themselves to interact with fellow associates during these times. Sometimes arrangements are made for the first day, but they are on their own after that. How could we turn this potential OW into a **WOW**? Maybe a different outgoing and friendly person could be assigned to take the new worker to lunch every day for their first week to alleviate that awkwardness and help them get to know more people in a shorter period of time. We all want to feel a sense of belonging within a group; that is what helps us get engaged. What a great way to help someone instantly feel as though they belong, without them having to "beg" for acceptance and companionship.

By the way, all of us want to contribute, but Millennials are especially team oriented and feel more "left out" than other generations of workers as a whole if not invited to participate and contribute. So, tap into their natural way of communicating and allow their collaborative creativity and teamwork to help the organization succeed.

One more thing about brainstorming is to *not* feel bad if we don't get immediate answers – or even workable ideas – at each session. The most important point to remember about brainstorming is that it is not about getting the right answers instantly; it is about prompting a dialogue. Once we begin to identify the questions we should be asking, we can then focus our efforts on finding answers to those questions. But if we are not asking the right questions – or any questions at all – we will never be able to move forward and create **WOW** experiences.

Brainstorming Techniques and Methods

There are many different methods of brainstorming that can help us organize our individual and collaborative ideas. Different methods work better than others for diverse situations and personality types. Here are three of the most popular:

Traditional Brainstorming. Traditional brainstorming is a great way to get many ideas and solutions, either individually or in a group setting. In this traditional method of idea generation, the goal is to obtain as many creative ideas from the group as possible, no matter how wild or impossible it may seem at the time. This is not the time to edit or stifle ideas. Just get them out and plan to go through each idea later to determine its feasibility to solve the problem.

Rules for brainstorming:

- Clearly define the problem.
- Stay focused on one problem during that session.
- No one criticizes or evaluates ideas during the brainstorming session.
- Everyone must try to contribute and develop ideas.
- Further develop other people's ideas, then use those ideas to create new ones – tag onto each other's ideas.
- Do not follow one train of thought for too long or get bogged down in logistics.
- Ask one person to capture the ideas on paper, which can then be distributed as a de-briefing memo to the involved associates.
- Have fun!

Traditional Brainstorming

*Problem:*_____

_____

_____

_____

_____

Ideas generated to solve the problem:

_____

_____

_____

_____

_____

_____

_____

_____

_____

_____

_____

_____

_____

_____

_____

_____

_____

_____

_____

_____

Mind Mapping. Mind Mapping is a method of organizing your thoughts as they come to you. The main topic is indicated in the center of a page; different sub-categories within that topic, as well as supporting points, stories, examples, and other content are listed around the main topic. As thoughts come to you, write them down in the appropriate place. Even if you don't know the appropriate place at that moment, just write it in a "miscellaneous" space and put it into a more appropriate location later. The point is to let the thoughts flow and get them down as quickly as possible so you don't lose them.

Mind-mapping

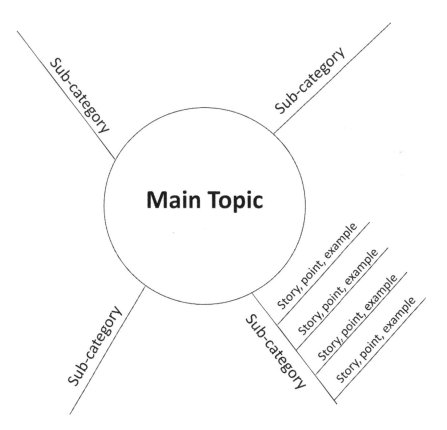

Mindstorming. The purpose of Mindstorming is to ask a question, and then write down 20 possible answers or solutions to that question. The point is not to stop before writing down 20 possibilities, no matter how crazy or stupid the answers may seem. This will force you to go deeper and get more creative than the surface answers that come easily at the start of the process.

*Question:*_____

_____

Answers:

1. _____
2. _____
3. _____
4. _____
5. _____
6. _____
7. _____
8. _____
9. _____
10. _____
11. _____
12. _____
13. _____
14. _____
15. _____
16. _____
17. _____
18. _____
19. _____
20. _____

Useless Meetings: Nothing is More Frustrating!

Why are meetings often met with dread and reluctance and deemed a waste of time? Because most of them are overly lengthy, repetitive, unfocused, unproductive and result in nothing but taking people away from critical tasks to do something that produces nothing. One of the worst things we can do with a meeting is make it a waste of time and effort where nothing is accomplished. The other factor to consider is that most meetings are not conducive for creative collaboration. The conference room may be very elegant, but it usually contains only a table with paper and pencils (maybe) on it and some chairs around it. It is quiet, dull . . . boring. We cannot expect people to file into a room like that, tell them to *"be creative!"* and then expect it to happen.

If we want to achieve **WOW** results from our meetings and brainstorming sessions, we need to change what our meetings normally look, sound and feel like. How do we get people excited and get their creative juices flowing for meetings? We must make them purposeful, productive and fun. This can be accomplished by following a few simple guidelines:

Make meetings purposeful

⊙ Communicate those objectives clearly before, during and after the meeting. Don't let anyone come to the meeting without knowing what they are there to accomplish. Don't let anyone leave it without knowing what you have achieved during your time together, as well as what you intend to accomplish after the meeting. Ensure that all team members know who is responsible for which tasks, when they are due, how progress and results will be measured, how they will be rewarded, and the reporting mechanisms for communicating those results to the rest of the team and the organization. Let them know as soon as possible if they have succeeded, or at least are progressing toward the goal identified in the meeting.

◉ Focus on results. Identify a specific result to be achieved by the meeting. Be sure everyone has a clear picture of what the desired result looks and feels like. Use stories, examples, photos – anything that can help project the image you want them to hold in their minds as they work toward the goal.

◉ Give them the "why." No one will embark upon a project enthusiastically without knowing why it is being requested. Give them the tie-in regarding how it contributes to overall company success, the customer experience, or their own personal success.

◉ Make sure they are productive.

   ✓ Create an agenda and stick to it. Keeping to a schedule not only allows people to plan accordingly, but it shows them you respect their time enough to stick to your stated agenda so they can plan the rest of their time properly.

   ✓ Set goals and priorities that align with the objectives and move the group forward so they can be achieved.

   ✓ Verify that everyone has a clear understanding of the goals and priorities, who is to carry out which piece of them, and by when.

◉ Identify and provide the tools available for them to use to accomplish the goal.

   ✓ For example, when solving a customer service problem, the tools could be the scripts our front-line people use, the customer service and service recovery policies we have developed, the flexibility in the rules and guidelines so associates can use their common sense when dealing with customers – and each other – and procedures they are to follow.

◉ Ensure everyone knows they are productive. Give periodic status updates on longer projects; report goals accomplished; give kudos and rewards; keep them focused on the goals; and hold celebration and recognition meetings when the overall objective is met.

◉ Decorate the room following a theme that lends itself to decoration. Or just select a theme for the meeting purpose by creating a tagline (e.g., "Beautify our lobby!" or "**WOW**ing up our speed of service!")

◉ Play music. Upbeat and energizing music adds energy and excitement to a room. Imagine how different it would be to come to the door of a meeting room that energized you, rather than one that was deathly silent.

◉ Have fun "props." Adult learning theory states that adults think best when they have something to do with their hands, so providing stress balls, fun props, unique writing utensils and paper, and other fun items will stimulate them to think better. Just don't provide noisemakers, or you may get nothing done over the racket!

◉ Have fun foods. Providing cookies, pizza, soft drinks or theme-related foods can stimulate the creative process, especially in the afternoon when adults normally experience a drop in their energy. One of my friends told me his wife receives many enthusiastic comments from her meeting attendees because she provides a bowl of candy at all of her meetings.

◉ Do interactive creativity exercises to keep team members from being bored and disengaged.

  ✓ Creative icebreakers to introduce team members to each other at the start of a project help get everyone involved right from the start.

✓ Starting each meeting with a fun fact, celebratory announce-
ment or recognition, or having each person tell a brief story
about something good that happened to them in the previous
week starts meetings off right, and sets a positive tone.

✓ If the group is large, breaking it into smaller groups to hold
discussions that are then reported to the larger group helps
give all attendees a chance to share ideas. It is also less
intimidating for some to speak in a smaller group than a
larger one.

◉ Allow those who are comfortable meeting in non-traditional
environments to do so with laptops in hand, talking, brainstorming, and generating ideas in a very relaxed, comfortable
setting. If this is not possible, try rearranging or replacing
furniture in a traditional setting to make it less traditional, or
transform the room's "look and feel" through décor or other
changes. Look at how you can make it more conducive to
creative work than the traditional sterile conference room.

◉ Find creative methods and outlets for sharing, rather than
relying solely on meetings. The Googleplex example of having
whiteboards in the halls is a great way to capitalize on
spontaneous and unplanned knowledge that crops up
unexpectedly. You may even get good suggestions from people
not formally on the team. One of my conference attendees put
heavy paper and crayons on the break room tables and
encouraged people to write down great ideas that spontaneously
occurred there. She called them "Crayola Cranium Bursts!"

◉ Change the format or time of the meeting. Some companies
have adopted "stand-up" meetings where all attendees stand
rather than sit down. This keeps the meetings shorter, changes
the flow, and eliminates the tendency to slouch, relax or become

tired or distracted. Other companies begin their meetings at noon to keep them as short as possible because attendees want to get to lunch. Find what works to change up the meetings enough to let everyone know they are different, succinct and productive.

Creating What-If Scenarios Through Negative Branch Reservation

One way to make the most of those brainstorming sessions, and help polish your proactive and critical thinking skills in the process, is called Negative Branch Reservation. It is a method of critical thinking that many scientists use to help them think of every possible thing that could go wrong, and create a way to avoid, mitigate or recover from it *before* it happens. In other words, whenever a new action is considered, there are reservations regarding the potential unintended negative consequences that could result from it. Therefore, we need to think about what-if scenarios and create plans and backup plans to prevent that negative result from happening, or keep its effects to a minimum.

Here's how it works: draw a diagram in which you put the new idea at the top of a page. Then draw a vertical line stretching below it to the bottom of the page, making a rudimentary "tree." Add horizontal lines for various "branches" of the tree that represent potential negative consequences of that action. Use this technique to brainstorm ways to prevent it from happening, thus trimming each negative branch from the tree. A sample diagram is shown below for your reference, and a template is included in the **WOW** Tools and Templates chapter.

For example, what if your department is planning to implement a new policy? In this exercise, you would try to think of all the negative branches that could occur, and find a way to eliminate or mitigate them. So, let's say a new policy is a little lengthy. What if associates won't read it all? Can you find a way to at least pull out all the pertinent parts as bullet points and put them on a cover page? (As a customer, I really wish that all those organizations that send me 16 pages of information in 8-point type would just tell me the basics of what I needed to know, and not bury it in all that legalese that covers *them*, but wastes my time and confuses *me*.) This trims the negative branch from the tree and lets you go on.

Now think of the next reservation: what if they don't understand it? What could we do to trim this branch? We could include examples and stories that illustrate the concept in action, or the desired results. This will trim that negative branch. The process continues until as many things as possible that could go wrong have been considered, and methods to eliminate them ahead of time discussed. These what-if scenarios can help prevent many of them from occurring at all. When I had a job as a systems analyst, I constantly used this type of exercise to create "what-if scenarios" and ensure that when one of our new programs went live, it didn't crash the entire system!

Negative Branch Reservation

Avoiding Groupthink

As we have learned, collaboration can be an effective exercise that generates ideas, hones them, makes processes better and helps develop teamwork and create organizational success. However, in any collaboration, we must be careful to avoid the phenomenon known as "groupthink," which is a term coined by social psychologist Irving Janis (1972). Groupthink occurs when a group makes faulty decisions because of certain group pressures. Groups affected by groupthink ignore alternatives and tend to take irrational actions.

A white paper on the website for Psychologists for Social Responsibility (http://www.psysr.org) describes groupthink, the symptoms of which are briefly outlined as follows*:

- The illusion of invulnerability, which creates excessive optimism and encourages members to take extreme risks.
- Collective rationalization, where group members discount warnings or fail to reconsider or confirm the validity of their assumptions.
- Belief in the inherent morality of the goal, in which members believe in the rightness of their cause and therefore ignore the ethical or moral consequences of their decisions. This gives rise to the noble but faulty decision that "the end justifies any and all means."
- Stereotyped views of the out-groups, where negative views of the "enemy" – within or outside of the group – make effective responses to conflict seem unnecessary. This is the true "us versus them" scenario, in which all *our* opinions are correct, and all *their* opinions are faulty.

---

*[Link to full article: http://www.psysr.org/about/pubs_resources/groupthink%20overview.htm]

- Direct pressure on dissenters, which puts tremendous pressure on group members to refrain from expressing arguments against any of the group's views.

- Self-censorship, which is a direct result of the pressure on dissenters not to argue. Therefore, if a group member even has doubts or small deviations from the *perceived* group consensus, they will not express them.

- Illusion of unanimity, which occurs as a result of the pressure on dissenters and self-censorship mentioned above. The majority views or judgments are assumed to be unanimous because no one is disagreeing with them. It may come to light later, in small or group discussions, that there were disagreements, but by then it is often deemed too late. If dissenters refrain from dissenting in the moment (during the meeting), they will certainly not bring up their disagreement at a future meeting, and call even more attention to themselves by doing so.

- Self-appointed "mindguards" who protect the group and the leader from information that is problematic or contradictory to the group's cohesiveness, view or decisions.

A group is especially vulnerable to groupthink when its members are similar in background, when the group is insulated from outside opinions, and when there are no clear rules for decision-making. Organizations can guard against groupthink by ensuring that team members are drawn from every level of the organization, as well as across departments. They should also represent a cross-section of various ages, cultures and life experiences. The ground rules must also be made very clear, so all members feel free to speak their mind to make the session as productive as possible.

WOWs in One Area Inspire WOWs in Other Areas

When you begin to do things differently, you will notice that when one area changes for the better, it flows over into other areas.

Case in Point:

The TSA in San Diego could have just put up the same old boring signs telling travelers the rules and regulations governing their behavior at the airport. Instead, they created a fun video that depicted beloved San Diego "characters," such as the Padres, San Diego Zoo animals and others, acting out what travelers should do as they passed through the security scanners. It was so interesting and humorous that I actually found myself wanting to stay in line longer to see the whole video!

As a result of placing a focus on making the communication of the rules so much fun, agents also focused on being more compassionate and fun. For example, as a family approached an agent checking IDs and boarding passes, the woman asked if he needed to see her ID, too, or just her husband's. At many airports, I've seen agents treat passengers disrespectfully and disdainfully for a lot less than that. But this agent didn't try to make her feel foolish for asking what he probably considered an obvious question. He joked with her as he told her he needed to see hers, too.

In addition, the designers of the building actually thought about how difficult it is to travel with luggage and drag it around, especially in the rest rooms (because you can't leave it unattended). When I visited the Ladies' restroom, I was amazed at how long and spacious the stalls were! No fighting with luggage, coats and stall doors. What a refreshing change!

You will know your workplace is turning into a **WOWplace** when it begins to look, sound and feel different from ordinary workplaces in many areas, not just one. Begin with one area.

What does your organization look like? Is it warm and welcoming? Comfortable, neat and clean? Is it well maintained? How are the rest rooms? Are they clean and neat? Does the equipment work? How about the break room? Is the microwave clean? Do workers clean up after themselves? Are workers dressed appropriately?

What does it feel like? Do visitors feel welcome? For that matter, do workers feel welcome, not only by the appearance of the physical building, but by their co-workers and every leader? Do they know their leaders? Do their leaders know them? Is everyone friendly? Do they get along? When disagreements occur, do they happen privately, rather than in public where they can cause discomfort? Are associates smiling and talking with customers? Is everyone being taken care of, with no one ignored?

What does it sound like? Is there laughter in the halls? Do people exude a good sense of humor? When they walk by each other, do they look up and smile? Do they greet each other? Are they usually smiling, or at least *not* scowling?

Look at each area of your company and find ways to bump them up, one at a time, until they have all been considered regarding where they fall on the **WOWplace** target. Are they an OW? Just OK? Really Good? Or a **WOW**? If they are not yet a **WOW**, find ways to bring them to that bull's-eye.

One of the best ways to do this is through the liberal use of humor.

Humor Abounds in the *WOWplace*

It is important to find the humor that exists all around us. Humor breaks down barriers. It eases stress. It can even reduce tension, because when anxiety and stress rise, we've just got to laugh or we'll probably scream, shout or cry. Personally, I prefer to laugh.

We have to laugh at the dumb things we do that we shake our heads at later, and sometimes we have to laugh at the things that other people do to us. Sometimes it is that someone has done something unintentionally that causes us stress, and other times we just have to get used to their idiosyncrasies because they are office mates or someone we may later need to work with on a project.

We all know when things get a bit too tense, because we say things like, *"I need a BREAK!"* or *"I need a vacation!"* When that happens, start looking for the humor in the situation because, as Milton Berle said, *"Laughter is an vacation!"* When you've had a good laugh with someone, doesn't it feel like you have gotten away from your problems for even just a few minutes? That is why we hear people saying, *"Thanks, I needed that!"* when we have given them a good laugh. It is like we've given them a little gift of laughter or a little vacation in the middle of a stressful day. That is not to say a big vacation isn't nice or necessary, but we all take little vacations whenever we laugh with other people. So try to take, and give others, a few instant vacations every day.

Make It a Habit to Respond With Humor

It may not be easy to do, but if we begin making it a habit of responding with humor rather than anger or frustration, at least some of the time, doing so starts to become progressively easier over time.

Think about a time when one thing went wrong and you handled it OK, but then something else went wrong right after that. The second response probably wasn't quite as controlled or unemotional as we would have liked it to be, but it wasn't too bad. But heaven help the person on the other end of the interaction when the third thing goes wrong. There is only so much we can take! The frustration either creeps up or piles in on us and we don't realize – or simply cannot control – how we respond. When this happens over and over on a daily basis, as it can in some high stress jobs such as front-line customer service, sarcasm, disbelief and negativity may become an automatic response that pops out of our mouth before we realize what we are saying or how we are saying it.

But if we make it a habit to look for and respond with humor, suddenly humorous things come out of our mouth, making everything a little easier to take, not only for us, but for everyone around us! My husband, Bruce, and I have gotten into this habit, and I think it is a big reason we were recently able to celebrate our 31st wedding anniversary! Of course, there are times when one or the other of us has to say, *"Will you please be serious?"* But I would rather have it *that* way than having to ask each other to *"lighten up!"*

Never Assume!

Bruce has also taught me another lesson over the last 31 years: Never assume that you can tell what another person is thinking or feeling. When we assume, we sometimes make the wrong assumption, and we misinterpret someone else's behavior simply because it differs from our own. Despite our constant belief to the contrary, we usually can't tell from outward appearances what is truly going on inside, so don't go there. We are all so different from each other. We act, speak, feel and think differently, and we all demonstrate our actions, reactions, and emotions in different ways.

One of the most difficult lessons for me to learn was that just because I show every emotion outwardly in a *big* way, it does not mean that if someone else doesn't act or react just as big, they are not feeling the same thing I am. They just don't express it the same way I do. There have been a few times when I've been telling a funny story during a presentation, but one person in the front row isn't laughing, or even reacting much at all. I remember wondering if I was reaching them at all. One of them later came to me and said, *"WOW, that was the funniest thing I ever heard!"* Really? You could have fooled me! Those comments pointed up how wrong my assumptions had been, and proves the point that you can't go by outward appearances. So, give people the benefit of the doubt, and don't jump to conclusions that could leave you feeling insulted or disrespected, or that could lead you to believe they are not taking a situation seriously. Sometimes that cover is really just a cover, and what is underneath is going full steam ahead.

Of course, sometimes we discover that a cover is all there is. I am reminded of the humorous book entitled *"Everything Men Know About Women"* by Cindy Cashman, writing under the pseudonym of Dr. Alan Francis: 100 pages, all completely blank! (I know, I know, but come on; *that's* funny!)

And that brings me to my next point.

Take Your Work Seriously, But Yourself Lightly.

We are all trying to do our very best every day on our jobs, and that means we sometimes take ourselves a little *too* seriously. We strive for perfection, but the harder we try, the more it eludes us. As a result, we are often overly critical of ourselves when we make a mistake, not to mention being too hard on others when *they* make them.

Learning to laugh at ourselves and our mistakes, rather than being excessively embarrassed or frustrated by them allows us to relax a bit and laugh at some of those dumb things we do. It also helps us become more realistic in our quest for – and expectation of – perfection, as we realize we are just not going to get there.

It really helps to remember that if we are not doing something dumb every once in a while, we are just not human! Obviously, this doesn't give us permission to slack off and justify unnecessary failures as just "being human and imperfect." But how much better would our workplaces be if we weren't always so stressed trying to be perfect, that we can't even try to be **WOW**?

Here is the upside to taking ourselves lightly: when we can admit that we've made a mistake, it not only humanizes us, but it gives us more credibility. If any of us are actually fooling ourselves into thinking that we don't make mistakes – or that no one notices them when we do – then we are in more serious trouble than we realize. This is never the case, and a leader can cause incredible damage to his reputation by pretending otherwise. We will not be able to gain and hold the trust of our colleagues if we don't realize and admit this truth.

Fun Starts at the Top

Taking this concept one step more, leaders can intentionally set the stage for an atmosphere of fun in the workplace.

***

Case in Point:

After having worked in more conservative corporate environments, partners John Powers and Catherine York of The Gilded Nut Snack Co., LLC in Portland, ME use the nutty titles of "Head Nut" and "Nut Pusher," instead of the more traditional titles normally used by executive leaders in most organizations.

In the same spirit of fun, many leaders in various types of companies have also taken the non-traditional title of "The Big Cheese!"

***

What tone of fun and creativity can little things like this set, when they start at the top and work their way down? I would love to work with these types of very successful leaders who take their work seriously, but are still able to take themselves lightly!

Don't Just Hope For Fun and Humor . . . Plan *For It!*

In fact, don't just learn to react with humor, plan to have fun each day so you don't have to rely on luck or happenstance to generate fun in your workplace. Build it right into the schedule! Some companies appoint an "Ambassador of FUN" each week or month! Others create an entire "Fun Committee" to be in charge of planning fun into each day or week. They brainstorm how to make one day per week more fun, as well as special occasions.

Have committee members ask the following questions: What can I laugh at today? What can we do to make someone else smile and enjoy themselves? Our co-workers? Our bosses? Our staff members? Visitors? Who is in dire need of a laugh so they can enjoy their day – and their job – a little more today and every day?

One nice way to make activities enjoyable and meaningful is to tie fun activities to charitable giving. Ideas such as each associate donating $1.00 for the privilege of dressing casually each Friday – or wearing a certain colored ribbon or dressing in a funny "costume" – and donating the funds to one or more designated charities, are very popular. As an added bonus to make it more meaningful for more people, find out which charities associates are connected with, and donate to different ones each month, rather than having the organization pick one charity without input from associates.

As Dale Carnegie always reminded us, people rarely succeed unless they are having fun in what they are doing. So, increase the success of your organization and everyone in it by allowing them to have fun while doing it.

How Can We Do Ordinary Things More Creatively?

Another way to put some fun back into our workplaces is to ask ourselves what tasks we do every day, and determine what the "normal" way is of doing that task. Then think of a better or more fun way to do it instead.

Case in Point:

During a long Skype video conference with a client, we all decided to take a 10-minute break and then come back and resume our meeting. All staff members on the call simply got up and left the room, leaving the webcam facing an empty chair.

But our client taught us an important lesson in fun that day. Before he left the room, he got a teddy bear from his office and put it in the chair in front of the camera so the rest of the meeting participants didn't have to look at a "boring" empty chair while he was gone. The bear had a sign taped to it that said, *"Jeff will be right back!"*

This tiny little act of humor brought a smile to my face, as well as to the faces of all the other participants!

What a fun way to be a little different, and bring even just a little bit more fun and joy to the meeting. It didn't cost a cent to do it; in fact, it usually doesn't! Displaying a fun side to our personalities where appropriate, even in business meetings, doesn't detract at all from our jobs. Instead, it connects us more strongly with the people who are working with us, and helps us build stronger relationships because they know they are working with a real person.

In addition to meetings, this concept can help in appropriate sales situations.

Case in Point:

A saleswoman once had to prepare for a big sales presentation. She wanted to find a way to make her presentation stand out from the crowd of experts who also had the opportunity to pitch their product to the prospective client.

So, she created a video for inclusion in her presentation. When it was her turn to present, she set the video up, passed out bags of popcorn and told the executives to *"enjoy the show!"*

When it came to decision time, she got the business because her presentation stood out in the minds of the executives.

[NOTE: Obviously, just setting up a flashy show was not going to replace the necessity to possess the expertise and product offerings to do the job effectively. In fact, all companies that were offered the opportunity to make a presentation to this group of executives had already been vetted, and made it to a shortlist of exceptional candidates. So, the playing field was level in terms of competence.]

That said, why did this presentation work? Because people – yes, even high-powered executives – like to have fun, since they are human, too. Everyone else who got the opportunity to make a presentation to this group did it in a very competent, but very "ordinary" way. The saleswoman mentioned above differentiated herself by making the *delivery* of her presentation memorable and creative, proving that when you can combine competence and credibility with fun and enjoyment, you can create an unbeatable combination!

Are We Creative?

It is easy to think and say the words, *"I'm pretty creative and open to new things."* However, just as it is very difficult to see disrespect and other negative impacts in our own actions, we sometimes think we are more creative than we actually are. For example, I once had a wonderful client who was open to many new ideas, and we have a great relationship.

At one point, we began working on a new website design for her. She told me she was very open to creative ideas and not married to any one idea. But when we began working together on a new design, we all discovered that the only one she liked was one that was already in her head. Since none of our outside ideas matched what she had already envisioned, we had to stop proposing new designs, figure out what she was picturing and create that.

What this lesson taught me was that it is OK to be creative in certain areas, but not in others. We don't have to go with new or different ideas in every area. In fact, it is advisable not to try to change too much at one time. It is too unsettling, difficult to control and hard to track and measure results. As I mentioned earlier in this chapter, let's not forget that we are not making changes or being creative just for the heck of it. We must have a reason for implementing the changes we are considering, such as improving associate morale, delivering better customer services, increasing sales, enhancing productivity, and a raft of other positive impacts we wish to put into effect.

So, think about how creative and open you really are. There are times when you just want things the way you want them...period. Again, that's OK. But honestly assess your views and opinions on new ideas, and decide where you actually fall on the "open to new ideas/not married to any one idea" spectrum in that particular instance. Communicate appropriately, and be sure your vision and purpose are clear. Then make changes in designated areas, one viable and logical step at a time when you are ready and prepared to do so. You will gain immense credibility by proceeding with creativity, innovation and fun if you implement change in a more organized fashion. Just because we are creative doesn't mean we have to be disorganized or wild and crazy! Your team will thank you for your honesty. Additionally, the clarity provided by being clear and organized before beginning the process will help everyone be more productive more quickly.

Being creative doesn't mean we have to be disorganized or wild and crazy!

How do we know how creative we really are, or should be? In addition to being aware of how we react to new ideas, whether we think of them ourselves or others propose them to us, there is a wonderful website called *MindTools* (www.MindTools.com) that contains a creativity quiz you can score immediately after taking the quiz online.

It is at the following link: http://www.mindtools.com/pages/article/creativity-quiz.htm.

Is It Worth It?

You may be asking yourself at this point, *"WOW, isn't this an awful lot of work?"* The answer is "Yes, it could be." It is not necessarily easy. But nothing worthwhile ever is. We can make the process as simple or as complicated as we wish. But isn't it worth it if we end up making a positive difference in the lives of our co-workers, our customers, our community or our families?

Think of it this way. Didn't we all get into business for a reason? Aren't we all going to work for a reason? Why are we where we are? Don't we want to have a positive impact on others? We all do things for our own reasons, and if we connect with those reasons we can remain positive as we strive toward a goal that is bigger than the everyday annoyances we run into as we continue on that path.

I heard a great quote one time, by an anonymous author: *"There are always two choices, two paths to take. One is easy, and its only reward is that it's easy."*

So, I ask you: do we really want to do things because they are easy? Or do we want to do things because they are worth it? The choice is up to us.

Chapter Summary:
How to WOW Through Innovation, Creativity and Fun

1. Give associates some sense of influence and control.
2. To think outside the box, there has to be a box! Start with the basics.
3. Break the norm and challenge the status quo.
4. Issue a bold challenge and ask associates to rise to meet it.
5. Be willing to do the extraordinary despite every excuse not to.
6. Get rid of the excuses.
7. Be flexible. If you can't change your situation, change your expectations.
8. Be transparent whenever and wherever possible.
9. Encourage collaboration as much as possible.
10. Use different collaboration techniques (brainstorming, mind mapping, mindstorming).
11. Get rid of useless meetings; make them purposeful, fun and productive!
12. Create "what-if" scenarios through Negative Branch Reservation.
13. Avoid "Groupthink."
14. Remember that **WOW**s in one area inspire **WOW**s in other areas.
15. Humor abounds in the **WOWplace**.
16. Make it a habit to respond with humor.
17. Never assume!
18. Take your work seriously, but yourself lightly.
19. Fun starts at the top.
20. Don't just hope for humor, plan for it!
21. Discover how you can do ordinary things more creatively.
22. Are we creative? Yes, but that doesn't mean we have to be disorganized or wild and crazy!
23. Is it worth it?

> *Rewards and recognition must be given in a multitude of ways, at planned and spontaneous times, and from expected and unexpected sources.*

Chapter Seven:

WOWplace Rule #5

A **WOWplace** is Rewarding

A **WOWplace** is Rewarding

There are many ways to make a workplace rewarding, but they cannot all relate to the paycheck. In fact, if we do not want our associates to be "all about the paycheck," then our reward systems cannot be all about that single factor, either. Rewards and recognition must be given in a multitude of ways, at planned and spontaneous times, and from expected and unexpected sources.

If we don't want associates to be "all about the paycheck," we cannot be all about it, either!

I am sure most of us have been in the position where we are making a good salary, but the atmosphere in the workplace is such that it is just not worth it. In some cases, no amount of money is worth the experience we must endure. On the flip side, there are some workplaces where the pay is not as high as we wish, but the mission, atmosphere, teamwork and leadership within the organization make it worth staying.

In other words, for **WOW**ers, staying engaged and excited about their work is not about money alone. Therefore, in order for a workplace to be considered a **WOWplace**, it must be personally, professionally *and* financially rewarding.

This is not big news. We all know it. But again, while we all know it, do we all *do* it . . . *consistently*? Do we place a strong focus on it so our culture demonstrates that we know what is important and are willing to do what is necessary to ensure our people never forget it?

Much of what was discussed in previous chapters is directly related to how we make our **WOWplace** emotionally and intellectually rewarding through respect, integrity, compassion, encouragement, creativity, inclusion and meaningful interaction at every level of the organization. A few more thoughts on these aspects of reward will be discussed in this chapter. But we will not go into laborious detail about how to create a Total Rewards package or plan, since there are many excellent books and articles available on these topics.

Instead, this chapter will discuss key concepts to help us creatively think about how our organization can offer categories of tangible and intangible benefits geared toward what associates want and need to help them succeed in all areas of their work and personal lives. These elements can then be included in a Total Rewards package that is right for the organization and its associates.

Associates will get – and stay – engaged, productive and loyal as long as they feel they are making an important contribution to the organization's success. It is an added benefit when the organization also helps them blend work and life duties so they experience less stress in trying to juggle the two, without having to make unreasonable or unacceptable sacrifices in either one.

Making It Personally Rewarding

Most of us do good works because we *want* to do them and because they make us feel good. We take pride in our work and our attitudes, and often cannot help ourselves because that is who we are. We want to produce the best work possible, not simply receive rewards or accolades. That said, isn't it awfully nice to get them once in a while anyway?

The harsh truth is that accolades in the workplace are often absent and good deeds ignored, while corrective "instruction" is almost never withheld. Because associates frequently need coaching or new direction when things go wrong, managers and supervisors are compelled to call them aside, say something about what happened and tell them how it might be corrected or avoided in the future.

Accolades are often absent and good deeds ignored, while corrective "instruction" is almost never withheld.

But when things go right, managers and supervisors often fail to praise associates for doing things well. Sometimes, they just don't think of saying anything, since nothing needs to be corrected. Other times, they are just too busy and cannot – or do not want to – take the extra time to go out of their way to offer what they consider "excessive" or unnecessary praise. Often, they believe that telling associates they are doing a good job once a year at performance review time is sufficient. Other leaders feel that giving kudos to associates is not required at all. They don't do it at home, their parents never did it for them, and they just do not see the need.

Nothing could be further from the truth. Research in this area is exploding with proof that companies that implement and practice giving formal and informal rewards and recognition consistently throughout the day – and throughout every level of the workplace – have more engaged associates who stay longer and are happier to contribute to the success of the team and the organization as a whole. In other words, when associates are happy, they want to create happiness and success all around them.

Foundational Elements for Engagement

Happiness, fulfillment and a feeling of contributing to something larger have become foundational elements for associate engagement, as these emotions drive personal and organizational pride and feed on themselves to create higher cycles of engagement at every level. In fact, as reported in a *Gallup Business Journal** article by Jerry Krueger and Emily Killham, research conducted by Daniel Kahneman, Ph.D. (professor of psychology and public affairs at Princeton University, and winner of the 2002 Nobel Prize in economics) revealed that *"Business is more about emotions than most businesspeople care to admit."*

Additionally, previous Gallup research, combined with other surveys conducted by the *Gallup Management Journal*, also reported that "a positive relationship with the supervisor has an important effect on engagement." (For more specific information on Kahneman's and other researchers' findings, please visit Gallup's article link: *http://businessjournal.gallup.com/content/20311/work-feeling-good-matters.aspx?version=print.)*

In fact, another very tangible demonstration of the impact of this positive relationship is the finding reported in the *Journal of Applied Psychology* that workers are less likely to miss work – even when their co-workers abuse paid leave – when they know their boss cares about them.

Leading By Example: Titled Leaders Are Not "Entitled" Leaders

What this means is that much more attention must be paid to supporting leaders at every level in their efforts to drive engagement, which means every leader must lead by example. In other words, *everyone* in the **WOWplace** must follow certain rules. The guidelines and limits of individual work-related rules may vary by individual and level within the organization. But if we want *all* associates to behave like leaders (whether or not they have an official title), we must all abide by the same rules of respect, civility and human compassion.

Titled leaders are not "entitled" leaders; they are not entitled to enforce rules they are not required (or willing) to follow.

One of the best ways to gain buy-in for any initiative at any level is for titled leaders to remember that they are not "entitled" leaders, behaving as though they are above the rules; no leader is entitled to enforce rules they are not required – or willing – to follow. So, for example, if there is an organizational rule that states, *"No one walks by a piece of trash on the ground without picking it up,"* leaders cannot walk by any trash they see on the ground without doing so, either. This concept correlates with those of organizational justice discussed in Chapter Three, as it is one more factor that contributes to associate engagement and perceptions of fairness in the workplace. Associates need to know that employers care enough about them to abide by whatever rules they impose on the rest of the organization.

Peer Level vs. Manager Recognition

Another factor that contributes to associate engagement and motivation is that of recognition and rewards for their efforts. While important research is being conducted on the effects of management and supervisory rewards and recognition, other critical research is being done on the impact of peer-level recognition. Researchers are asking, *"Which is better: recognition from peers, or recognition from leaders?"* The findings conclude that both are important, but even though it is vitally important for leaders at every level to participate in the recognition process, associates usually report feeling more appreciative of recognition offered by their peers.

There are a couple of crucial reasons why this distinction exists. First, peers know what each other are doing on a daily basis. When they say "thank you," the impact is much more meaningful because it is more specific and personal. Therefore, the person receiving recognition knows it is heartfelt and based on real actions and impacts. This principle also applies to praise from direct supervisors, who work closely enough with associates to know the specific impact of their actions.

In contrast, what happens with executive-level recognition is that the "thank you" is often perfunctory or vague. The associate does not know if the executive is really aware of what they did and its impact on the organization, or if the leader is just reading a "script" that offers lip service for a vague "job well done." Consequently, this type of recognition from leaders has less impact than the *real* praise they receive from those who appreciate the actual act.

Two bodies of research offer insight into how this situation can be corrected. The first is that of Daniel Kahneman, Gallup and other researchers, whose findings illuminate the importance of leader recognition in coaching and spurring associates to higher success. The second is that of other researchers, whose findings demonstrate the enormous impact of peer or direct supervisor recognition that focuses on the specific strengths and actions of associates. When these two critical findings are analyzed together, it is clear that when managers and executives *do* thank associates, their comments must address specific accomplishments about which the executive has fairly detailed knowledge.

To state it more succinctly: *if you can't say something specific and meaningful, don't say anything at all.*

The big *"ah-ha"* is that recognition from executives has the capacity to be much more meaningful if done right, because it is perceived as genuine and more heartfelt.

However, there is another reason why it is important for leaders to offer specific praise to associates at every level. Since it is so unusual for detailed associate actions to come to the attention of high-level executives who have much bigger issues to think about on a daily basis, it is that much more meaningful when busy executives take the time and effort to personally thank an individual associate for a specific effort. When this occurs, the associate feels more valued and important to the success of the organization because their actions were worthy of being brought to the attention of a highly-ranked executive.

An added benefit is that this can have a tremendous "ripple" effect of gratitude and engagement. Once meaningful recognition is received by an executive, any *astute* associate must realize that their actions were brought to the executive's attention by someone else. If the executive is sensitive enough to let the associate know who told them about it (usually the associate's supervisor or manager), the associate feels gratitude toward the person responsible for bringing it to the executive's attention. This selfless act of recognition strengthens the bond between supervisor and associate, further increasing engagement and loyalty.

The Problem with Formal Reward Systems

Obviously, there must be formal reward systems in place, such as performance reviews, raises and periodic award celebrations. But if these systems do not occur more than once a year, it may be too late for the review to make its intended impact.

For example, an associate working on a large, complex goal is often given no guidance, reinforcement or encouragement throughout the year regarding whether or not they are moving in the right direction and completing the appropriate tasks on time. This could allow them to go too far off course before being told *at their annual review* that they were not heading in the right direction all year, and consequently have already failed. Therefore, just as with team projects and goals, periodic individual goal reviews and progress reports should be implemented to help guide and incrementally encourage or correct the associate, increasing their likelihood of success.

The Need for Informal Reward Systems

Leaders cannot be everywhere at once, nor should they have to be. In order to ensure that associates at every level remain connected to their organization and goals, and to ensure that they feel important and valued every day, informal reward systems must also be implemented.

Many organizations have put informal and spontaneous reward systems in place to enable others to give associates surprise accolades.

Case in Point:

At one of my programs, an attendee began tracing his hand on a piece of paper as we were discussing informal reward systems. When he was done, he raised his hand, waved the paper in the air, and told us what they did at his company:

When they see someone who has done something great, they take a piece of paper, trace their hand on it, date it, write the name of the associate they want to praise, as well as what they did to earn that praise, and sign it. They then hand the paper to the associate to give them a "pat on the back."

WOW! Simple, easy, instant, spontaneous, creative and meaning-ful, and it costs the company virtually nothing to do. This concept can be used in any format that fits your organization and culture: paper, phone, e-mail, text, tweet or apps. Many hotels have reward systems that also allow guests to compliment associates by filling out a paper, giving them a badge or sticker. Badges and stickers are conveniently placed throughout the property so guests have easy access to them any time they feel the urge to give praise. Other types of businesses have similar recognition vehicles enabling customers to praise exceptional associates.

To assist with your spontaneous reward efforts and demonstrate how easy it is to implement a similar system in your organization, I have created a free template for 4x6 **WOW** index cards that thank people for their **WOW** actions. The front contains the words *"Thanks for your WOW!"* The back has room for the giver to write a note to the recipient. The cards look like this:

To:_____	
From:_____	
Date:_____	
Thanks for:_____	

Front of card   *Back of card*

You can get these cards in one of two ways:

⊙ Download the free template (designed for 4x6 index cards) at the following link, and print on your own blank cards: *www.sandygeroux.com/WOW-Thanks-index_cards.pdf.*

⊙ Order convenient and cost-effective packs of pre-printed cards from our online store: *http://shop.sandygeroux.com.*

Share The Love!

When you make associates feel important and valued inside the workplace, they feel better about themselves and their jobs. Taking this concept a step further, when you can connect even more emotionally by making them feel proud in front of their family members and others *outside* of the work community, you create an incomparable **WOW** that just cannot be forgotten or overlooked!

My friend and speaking colleague Dave Timmons, a "Leadership Artist" who speaks on the art of emotional leadership, shares with his audiences this story of how a tip he learned from his mentor created a **WOW** with one of his associates. Dave has graciously allowed me to relate it here.

Case in Point:

Jennifer was a good associate on my team. During a special project that Jennifer was assigned to, she went over and beyond for several weeks and came up with an idea that solved several major issues for our team and company. Instead of the usual movie tickets and recognition in the newsletter, I got approval to reward Jennifer with $100.

Here's the cool part: instead of giving Jennifer the $100, I bought a $100 gift card from Jennifer's favorite place to shop, Ann Taylor Loft. I then bought a very nice "Thank You" card and mailed the gift card to Jennifer's home, addressed to her husband and three small daughters. The note inside the card read as follows:

Dear Randy, Emily, Elizabeth, and Maggie,

Your wife and mom is AWESOME! She works so hard for our team and we really appreciate her enthusiasm and ideas. On my behalf, would you kindly present her with this gift card for being such a great teammate at our company? She deserves it!

Thank you all for sharing Jennifer with us during the day.

Warmest Regards,
Dave Timmons, Senior Vice President

How much better do you think it made Jennifer feel to have this great compliment and gift from her manager (already a **WOW**) amplified by sending it to her husband and children, and allowing *them* to see how great she was and join in the lovefest? Associates' family members often have no idea of what their loved ones do on the job, how great a job they are doing, or how much they are appreciated by others in the organization. By involving family members in the rewards and recognition process, it adds another layer of pride and respect for the associate, and inspires them to continue creating successes for themselves and the company.

Appreciation Flows Both Ways

One important and often overlooked fact to remember is that appreciation flows both ways.

Leadership training programs always stress the importance of leaders recognizing and rewarding great work, fantastic attitudes and an excellent work ethic in the people they supervise. But how often do leaders ever receive *any* kind of informal appreciation from others?

Case in Point:

An Administrative Professional I once met works for the head doctor of a large medical practice. Most workers in the practice are intimidated by him and his position. But because she works directly for him, she has an opportunity to see and comment upon his kindness and actions more often than others who are not in that position. Every once in a while she writes a note about something she really appreciates about him or something he did. While you may assume that this would mean nothing to such an important and highly placed man in the organization, he prizes these notes so highly that he brings them home to show his wife!

Associates in lower level positions may be intimidated by a leader's position and feel uncomfortable giving praise upward, especially to those at much higher levels of the organization. But leaders in higher level positions are often the ones who give and receive the least amount of praise. This could be a contributing factor in a leader's tendency to forget or dismiss the impact of appreciation and praise. It may also justify their feelings and attitudes reflected in the statements, *"I don't get any praise and I'm doing just fine!"* and *"If it's good enough for me, it's good enough for them!"*

The problem with these statements and beliefs is that although leaders are usually adequately rewarded monetarily for their efforts, studies reveal that compensation is actually not first on the list of top job attributes. The top attributes involve being valued, appreciated, and listened to, which means that any human leader must also desire them.

So, the next time you see an appropriate opportunity to let any leader in your organization know how much you appreciate something they just did – or even what they do on a regular basis – say something about it. If we start reminding all leaders of how good it feels to receive small acts of appreciation *from* others, it may inspire them to do it more often *for* others, as well.

Making it Professionally Rewarding

One of the best ways an organization can reward its associates is by helping them improve their current skills and learn new ones. Consistent on-the-job training is necessary for workers to perform their jobs adequately. However, we must never underestimate the added value provided by offering supplemental training programs in addition to the basic skills and requirements for the job. Soft skills training including, among others, areas of leadership, communication, negotiating, delegating and emotional intelligence, enhances any worker's ability to perform their job at the highest level of performance and productivity. Remember that almost every executive works their way up to their current position using valuable hard and soft skills acquired in various positions, and at various companies, along the way.

Therefore, it is up to the organization to remain competitive by keeping technology, business practices and tools current – even cutting edge – so workers keep their skills at the highest possible levels. As much as some associates balk at having to learn new technology and skills, offering these opportunities accomplishes several positive goals, including:

- ◉ Identifying workers who are willing to learn and grow, separating "the wheat from the chaff" in terms of future leadership candidates. If someone is not willing to learn and grow in an entry- or mid-level position, how solid is their leadership capacity?

- ◉ Enabling the organization to remain competitive by providing workers with tools and incentives for creating innovative products, getting potential buyers to purchase these products and keeping those customers loyal after the sale.

- ◉ Helping the organization attract and retain top talent. The people who want to work for companies on the rise, rather than those content to rest on past successes.

- ◉ Benefiting workers in their personal lives. Leadership, communication and other skills they learn in the workplace are also applicable in everyone's personal life.

- ◉ Offering ambitious workers valuable opportunities to remain viable in an increasingly competitive job market and build a successful career in their current and future organizations.

One quick comment regarding any concern about providing associates with training that will benefit them in their current position, but may also cause them to be more marketable at another company: we all know that most associates will not be with the same organization for life, regardless of whether or not we give them additional training. Do it anyway. Giving people the training they need to succeed anywhere not only makes them more effective in their current position, enabling us to reap the benefits while they are with us, but it also engenders feelings of loyalty because they know their organization cares about them, which may entice them to stay with us longer and engage at a higher level.

Once again, if organizations *go first* and prove they are not just looking for "what's in it for me," showing that they also care about their workers, workers will stop looking *only* for "what's in it for them" and begin to care more about the organization in return.

Mentoring Programs

For many companies, mentoring programs are a valuable method to engage associates. Not only do they reinvigorate experienced workers who may feel stagnation in their current jobs, but they allow newer workers to feel a greater connection and appreciation for an organization that goes to much greater lengths than most to help them grow.

Formal and informal mentoring programs exist in too many forms to explain in detail here, but below are a few formats with brief descriptions of each:

One-on-One Mentoring: one mentor to one mentee.

Useful for improving interpersonal skills such as leadership, communication, delegation and conflict management; personal and work/life issues; guidance and advice from senior associates on navigating the corporate ladder, and advice from those with global experience, or more senior experience and expertise.

Very useful for: helping associates grow and develop personally and professionally.

Peer Mentoring: one-on-one relationship that occurs between co-workers within the same peer group, grade level, or job series; could encompass a full (small) organization.

Very useful for: facilitating colleagues' professional growth and mutual learning, and building a sense of community.

Situational Mentoring: short-term relationship, usually between one mentor and one mentee; can transition to a long-term relationship if both parties agree.

Very useful for: acclimating new associates more quickly and addressing short-term individual and team needs; "just-in-time" assistance.

Group Mentoring: one mentor and a group of mentees or protégés; the group fosters sharing of experiences with all group members – not just the mentor – sharing insights.

Very useful for: helping a group of associates interact and learn at one time.

Mosaic (Team) Mentoring: more than one mentor and either one mentee or a group of mentees. Mentors communicate regularly and work together or separately with mentee(s) to help them reach identified goals.

Very useful for: leadership development and executive succession planning.

Mentoring Circles: typically consist of two mentors and five mentees (one senior level mentor, one business unit manager or director and five peer mentors).

Very useful for: creating and improving diversity initiatives and providing mentees with advice from multiple levels and mentors.

Reverse Mentoring: Mentoring of a senior person (in terms of age, experience or position) by a junior person, especially in the fields of technology, computing and Internet communications. (NOTE:

successful reverse mentoring requires the ability to break down the barriers of status, power and position.)

Very useful for: helping associates learn new skills.

Flash Mentoring: Participants meet one-on-one for one hour or less to share advice and lessons learned; after the first meeting, both decide if they should continue.

Very useful for: quick sharing and determining "fit," and helping executives and senior staff with little time to mentor others.

Virtual (Online) Mentoring: one-on-one mentoring online via teleconferencing, Internet or e-mail.

Very useful for: personal and professional growth when mentoring cannot be done in person, or as an additional resource without using in-person resources.

Supervisory Mentoring (coaching): ongoing one-on-one help and guidance that is done on the job, as part of the supervisor's job.

Very useful for: serving as a routine part of the job of helping associates grow.

When done properly, mentoring can improve morale and performance, promote professional development and reduce learning time and cost. In addition, it can also increase company cohesion, increase associate engagement and loyalty, help with succession planning and retention of high performers, as well as helping address diversity issues. It can also help close the "gap" between the top and the bottom, especially in large organizations, by providing a way for newer workers to gain access to higher level and more experienced workers – an opportunity especially prized by younger workers of the Millennial generation. Take a look at the following statistics:

Minority workers who have advanced the farthest have a strong network of mentoring relationships.

> *This is also true for the advancement of women to senior positions.*
> - Harvard Business School
>
> *Expert mentors can double an associate's success.*
> - Mick Mortlock, Co-Founder, Intel University
>
> *77 percent of companies credited mentoring with increasing associate retention and performance.*
> - Business Finance Magazine

Many resources are available to help companies create and improve their mentoring systems. Find one that is right for your organization and take incremental steps to implement a formal or informal mentoring system for your associates.

Making It Financially Rewarding

It is common knowledge that associates get paid to do a job, and any work products developed while employed at the company belong to the company. But if an associate develops something that brings an incredible new product to market, or creates a significant increase in sales or profits, why wouldn't the organization engage in a little "profit-sharing" to thank that person?

This can be accomplished in many ways, including:

⊙ Paying a one-time bonus.

⊙ Giving a gift card personalized to the person's tastes. Don't just give everyone a standard gift card to one local restaurant or store. What if they don't like that type of food, or don't wear that type of clothing? Find out what they do like, and give them a gift card that has personal meaning and value for them.

⊙ Holding weekly/monthly/quarterly pool parties, pizza parties or other parties tailored to what your co-workers enjoy). Hold "friendly competitions" between individuals and teams; reward the ones who create the highest results. Be sure to tie rewards to performance and profits. Giving rewards for meaningless actions that do nothing to advance sales or profits will reduce a company's success, not to mention de-motivating the team. Let the team know how their efforts enabled the organization to succeed so they feel rewarded and recognized for their participation in important work efforts.

Other Types of Rewards

There are also many non-traditional ways to make working at a particular organization rewarding. Every year, MetLife conducts a study of Associate Benefits Trends that reveals very interesting information about new traditional and non-traditional rewards, including innovative ways to allow workers to accomplish their tasks and achieve their personal and professional goals.

The entire report can be found at the following link: *https://www.metlife.com/assets/institutional/services/insights-and-tools/ebts/ml-10-Annual-EBTS.pdf.*

It contains several important insights that can be used to position an organization to attract and retain talent, and help create higher retention and engagement, including several summarized as follows:

⊙ Non-medical benefits such as life, dental, disability and vision coverage are significantly more important to workers than they have been in the past.

⊙ Due to potential holes in the Medicare system, most employers recognize the need and responsibility to help associates achieve financial security, not necessarily through higher employer expenditures, but through expanded retirement programs, financial wellness education and planning, and debt reduction advice. In fact, 63 percent of workers realize a need for greater personal responsibility in this area, but are looking for support and help from employers with this challenge.

⊙ Associates want employers to arrange for a wide variety of voluntary programs for which associates will pay on their own. These include traditional products such as long-term health care, critical illness insurance, optional life and disability insurance, and other insurance to fill gaps in coverage and benefits. They also include non-traditional products such as legal services that help with identity theft, will preparation and adoption, as well as wellness programs.

⊙ Associates may not yet be more loyal to employers overall, but they are depending on employers to provide more benefits at an earlier age, causing them to stay longer.

⊙ Informing workers of a plan to maintain benefits is helpful, as the study reveals that although only 10 percent of employers are planning benefits cuts, 33 percent of workers are expecting their employer to do so.

Two *Business Management Daily* reports* also confirm many of the above findings and add several factors that help cure absenteeism, which by definition improves associate engagement. They also indicate several flex trends that will likely affect organizations when

---

*This information is proudly provided by *Business Management Daily.com* at the following links:
http://www.businessmanagementdaily.com/33159/formal-policies-flex-help-cure-absenteeism#_
http://www.businessmanagementdaily.com/31761/8-flex-trends-that-will-affect-your-company

trying to attract and retain top talent going forward:

1. **Flextime and telework are the new normal.** Even if this type of work cannot be accommodated full-time, allowing workers to employ these methods to accomplish their work tasks allows them the ability to take care of personal business while still accomplishing their necessary work duties.

2. **More associates are turning to EAPs** for help with personal problems. Almost three-quarters of employers have associate assistance programs, up from 46 percent in 2005.

3. **Elder-care leave and assistance is catching up** with child care as a popular work/life benefit. More than 40 percent of employers in the survey provide information about elder-care services, offer resource and referral programs or offer DCAPs for elder care.

4. **More employers value volunteerism.** About 20 percent give associates time off to volunteer, and more than 80 percent of those make that paid leave.

5. **Employers are adopting new metrics.** They are more willing to measure associates' value by what they accomplish, not the hours they put in.

Implementing these types of programs shows workers that employers care not just about what associates do for the organization, but about the associates themselves.

Ask Your Associates

In light of the many options available to recognize and reward the associates in each individual organization, a company's first step may be to conduct an associate survey to gauge their engagement level, as well as where their associates' interests lie.

One important caution about surveying associates is to ensure that there is a plan for what to do with the feedback, and that associates know what to expect. The worst thing an organization can do is to survey associates, allow them to believe there is a purpose for the survey, but then do nothing with the feedback received. Many valid reasons exist for conducting surveys, such as:

- Improving or maintaining current benefits.
- Offering new benefits.
- Creating a positive culture that involves them in decision-making where possible.

However, if your organization is planning to conduct a survey, be sure leaders are prepared to act on the results.

Create a Culture of Caring

The most important thing to remember is that it all works if we care about each other and express it. Stories and acts of appreciation often go unrecognized. But just as in our personal lives, although people may *know* we care about them, it is really good to *hear* it occasionally.

Chapter Summary:
How to WOW by Making the WOWplace Rewarding

1. Making it personally rewarding.
   a. Accolades in the workplace are often absent and good deeds ignored, while corrective "instruction" is almost never withheld.
   b. Foundational elements for engagement.
   c. Leading by example: titled leaders are not "entitled" leaders.
   d. Peer level versus manager recognition.
   e. The problem with formal reward systems.
   f. The need for informal reward systems.
   g. Share the love!
   h. Appreciation flows both ways.
2. Making it professionally rewarding.
   a. Training.
   b. Keeping up with current technology, business practices and tools.
   c. Mentoring programs.
3. Making it financially rewarding.
   a. Bonuses.
   b. Gift cards.
   c. Weekly/monthly/quarterly team rewards.
   d. Other types of rewards: traditional and non-traditional benefits and programs.
   e. Ask your associates.
   f. Create a culture of caring!

Providing associates with tools and templates

helps them succeed by giving them a framework

and "guide" to achieve your mutual goals.

Chapter Eight:

WOWplace Tools and

Templates

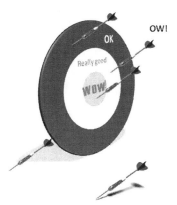

[8]

WOWplace Tools and Templates

All of the tools and templates mentioned in this book have been assembled in this chapter for your convenience in finding and using them to help you turn your workplace into a **WOWplace**.

Please use and share them liberally to create **WOW** experiences for everyone in your organization.

For electronic versions of these tools, please visit our website (www.theWOWplace.com) and click on the Tools tab.

Target the **WOW**!

Current Scenario:_____

_____

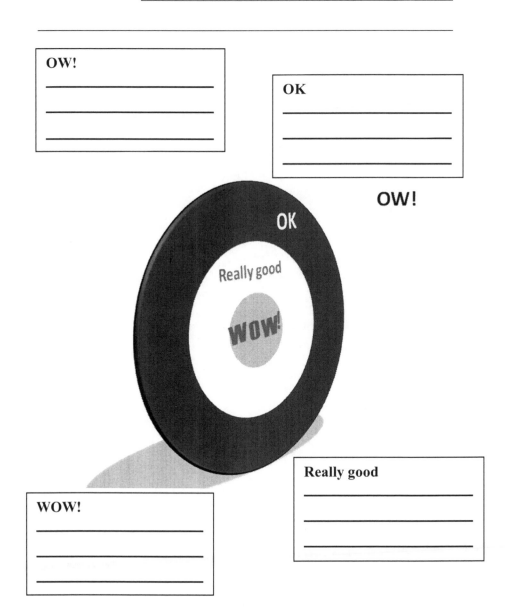

OW!
_____
_____
_____

OK
_____
_____
_____

OW!

Really good
_____
_____
_____

WOW!
_____
_____
_____

Anatomy of the WOW

Event/Event Phase	WOW Impact: Customer Experience	WOW Impact: Associate Experience	WOW Impact: Supervsor/ Manager Experience	WOW Impact: Company Experience/ Rep.

The 1-2-3s of Doing More Than Appease

Question #1: What can I do now?

_____

_____

_____

_____

_____

_____

Question #1: What else *can I do now?*

_____

_____

_____

_____

_____

Question #1: What else can I do later *. . . or* for *later?*

_____

_____

_____

_____

_____

Traditional Brainstorming Template

*Problem:*_____

_____

_____

_____

_____

Ideas generated to solve the problem:

_____

_____

_____

_____

_____

_____

_____

_____

_____

_____

_____

_____

_____

_____

_____

_____

_____

_____

_____

_____

Mind-Mapping Template

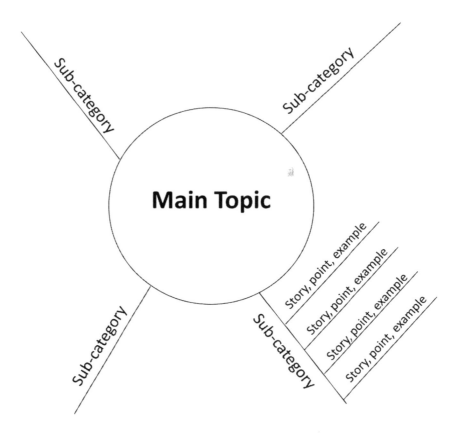

Mindstorming Template

*Question:*_____

_____

Answers:

1. _____
2. _____
3. _____
4. _____
5. _____
6. _____
7. _____
8. _____
9. _____
10. _____
11. _____
12. _____
13. _____
14. _____
15. _____
16. _____
17. _____
18. _____
19. _____
20. _____

Negative Branch Reservation Template

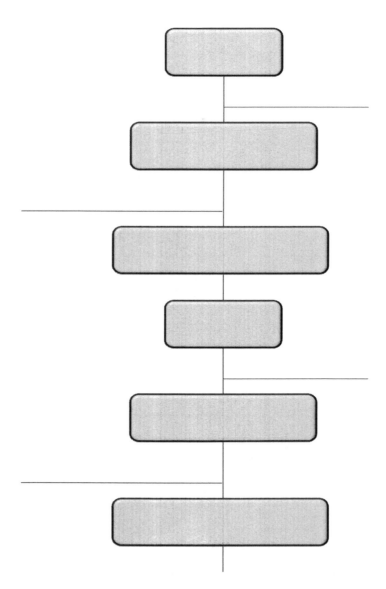

WOW Thank You Cards

To:_____

From:_____

Date:_____

Thanks for:_____

_____

_____

_____

Link to electronic (full color) file:
www.sandygeroux.com/WOW-Thanks-index_cards.pdf

*Creating a **WOWplace** requires action. Make a plan: start with baby steps, keep moving forward, and commit to creating **WOW** experiences.*

Chapter Nine:

Your Call to Action

[9]

Your Call to Action

Turning your workplace into a **WOWplace** may take some time, depending on your organization's current levels of engagement and morale. Don't be discouraged if it doesn't happen overnight. Nothing worthwhile ever does.

If your organization is well on its way to becoming a **WOWplace**, it may only take a short time to move *all* your actions from "Very Good" to **WOW** – and keep them there. If it's not there yet, it may take a few weeks or months to generate, build or re-build the trust needed to engage associates' hearts and minds, get them to take ownership of *every* situation and proactively think of how to create **WOW**s. But if you commit to instilling a focus on creating the **WOW** into your culture, so everything is done with the following question in mind: *"Will this create an OW or a **WOW**?"* it *will* happen over time.

Above all, place the greatest emphasis on *going first* when it comes to showing respect for everyone at every level. This one factor may be *the* greatest differentiator between whether or not your organization remains a workplace or becomes a **WOWplace**.

It is my hope that this book has sparked many new ideas and mindsets to assist your organization in moving forward by creating **WOW** experiences for associates and customers alike . . . all of which will help you turn *your* workplace into a **WOWplace**.

219

ABOUT THE AUTHOR

Sandy Geroux, M.S., is a recognized authority on creating **WOW** experiences for customers and associates alike. Her presentations focus on the impact of everyday, consistent actions that add up to exceptional experiences for everyone around us.

Since 2000, she has spoken to diverse audiences, helping leaders at every level inspire associates and co-workers to eliminate excuses, share their ideas and knowledge and go the extra mile to find the *hidden* WOW's that foster higher levels of customer service and employee engagement.

She lives in Orlando, Florida, with her husband of 31 years.

FOR MORE INFORMATION

If you'd like to book Sandy for a keynote, breakout or training program for your company, please visit her website, where you will find details on her key points, testimonials from past clients, calendar, and more information than you probably want to know!

Sandy's website address is:
www.theWOWplace.com

Or you can call or e-mail her at:
(407) 856-1188 / sandy@theWOWplace.com)

~

Sandy also has many free resources, including:

Sandy's blog containing quick tips on creating WOW experiences. She'd love for you to subscribe and comment on her posts any time you wish to share your WOW insights with others:

www.WOWplace.com

~

Sandy's FaceBook page, containing program updates, great comments, and more links to information Sandy loves to share information that inspires others:

www.FaceBook.com/wowplace

~

Social Media

Sandy is also on:
Twitter (@SandyGeroux)
LinkedIn
Google+
Google Hangouts
YouTube